What others are saying about *The Live Launch Method*

"Kelly Roach's Live Launch Method is a massive pattern interrupt that turns upside down everything you thought you knew about building your business online—in the best possible way. A MUST read for anyone doing business online!"

~ Ali Brown

Entrepreneur, Founder & CEO of The Trust Network

"Having the components to the Live Launch Method at my fingertips every day has been such a GIFT in my business. Utilizing this method helped me create over $230K in five months with more ease, grace, fun, and connection than anything else I have ever used. Do yourself a favor and step away from the old school methods of selling that leave you feeling pushy and disconnected from the people you serve and dive into this book today. You won't regret a moment, and you might just change your life."

~ Kelly Ruta

CEO of Kelly Ruta International and Founder of The Becoming Limitless Program

"If you don't know Kelly, follow Kelly, and love learning from Kelly, it's time to start. Kelly's created a launch strategy that is not only simple and effective, but groundbreaking in so many ways. She's created a path for *anyone* to engineer six-figure plus launches, regardless of their starting point. For those tired of the old ways of launching, she's breathed new life into the process, making seven-figure leaps in your business more within grasp than it's ever been. Whether you are just starting

out or have been running a multi-million-dollar company for years - this book is without a doubt, a MUST read."
~ Jennifer Allwood
Business Coach and Author, Fear Is Not the Boss of You

"Kelly Roach is my go-to gal on how to create a six- and seven-figure launch, and this book is further proof that she is the master of her craft. The Live Launch Method is like a dance between foundational business principles and social media marketing, so you have a full understanding of how to use this revolutionary process to get the biggest results. I know that next time I launch a program, I'll be going back to this book again and again for all of Kelly's incredible wisdom."
~ Cathy Heller
Host of the "Don't Quit Your Day Job" Podcast

"Kelly Roach and *The Live Launch Method* have shaken things up with what most entrepreneurs teach about digital marketing. It is refreshing to see someone zigging when everyone else is zagging. Now more than ever, we need to be innovating in our small businesses. This book is a must read. You will not be disappointed."
~ Stacy Tuschl
#1 International Best-selling Author and Host of the "Foot Traffic" Podcast

"This book is literally handing you your million-dollar marketing strategy! Kelly's Live Launch system **works**. Her ability to explain what to do is step-by-step, highly inspiring, and easy to understand. Kelly's Live Launch Method shows you how to grow your business to as big as you can dream of it being. I can't wait to keep implementing everything Kelly teaches in these pages!"

~ Kendall SummerHawk
Creator of the #1 Coach Training School Where Women Become Certified Business & Money Coaches

"Kelly's *Live Launch Method* book couldn't be more needed in a time where we need to rethink how we do business. Kelly's method is based on the fundamentals of building relationships, breakthroughs, and intimacy with an audience despite shortened attention spans. Our people crave connection and need our services but can't tell the difference between just a nice brand and services that actually produce results. Business owners more than ever need to look for ways to create connection and trust without wasting time, effort, and marketing dollars on crazy complex funnels. Kelly and her team are well poised to help any small business owner embrace and deploy social selling and the Live Launch Method with a proven model that can help you create seven-figure income streams in your business."

~ Michelle Bosch
Real Estate Investor and Co-Creator of the Land Profit Generator Program

The Live Launch Method

The Simplicity Meets Strategy Formula to Make Millions Online

By Kelly Roach

Business Growth Strategist | Educator | Peak Performance Coach

The Live Launch Method
The Simplicity Meets Strategy Formula to Make Millions Online

Independently published

ISBN: 978-0-578-67118-5

Cover design by Alisha Whaley

To all of my students: Thank you for dreaming big dreams, believing in yourself and taking action to make your vision a reality. You inspire me beyond belief each and every day.

About Kelly Roach

Kelly Roach transforms overworked entrepreneurs into seven-figure CEOs. With her Executive Fortune 500 experience and results, Kelly combines timeless business principles employed by billion-dollar corporations with the speed and agility of the most powerful online marketing strategies of today.

Kelly's company, the Unstoppable Entrepreneur is the leading online business coaching program in North America today. Leveraging scalable intimacy to create the first-ever accountability-driven coaching program on the market, while revolutionizing the way entrepreneurs launch their offers, Kelly's company has catapulted into the multi-millions while helping entrepreneurs around the globe do the same.

In addition to being a best-selling author, Kelly is also an ongoing expert on ABC, NBC, Fox, and The CW. She has been featured in some of the world's leading publications including *Inc.* and *Forbes* and is the host of the Top 50 Marketing podcast, "The Unstoppable Entrepreneur Show."

Kelly is committed to ongoing philanthropic work, with a 1:1 business model that brings clean drinking water to those who do not have access through her Human Family Foundation.

In addition to running her coaching company with a team of 20 full-time employees (and growing), Kelly is the co-founder of a second company, Give Her Courage, The Courageous Brand. Kelly founded this company to create a movement designed to give young girls the competitive edge they need to rise to the top, break through barriers, and create lasting change in the world.

Table of Contents

Introduction

Congratulations for taking the first step – picking up this book – to learn how you can make your business an unparalleled category of one in your space. The Live Launch Method is not just about making ridiculous amounts of money in your business but also about making a difference and building a brand reputation that precedes you.

I am excited to take you through this process, so you can become the next Live Launch Method superstar, changing your life and achieving financial freedom. This process has already changed the lives of thousands of entrepreneurs around the globe, and my goal in writing this book is to help you join those ranks.

No matter which industry you serve, you can only achieve the growth you want for your business when you are able to scale it... and scale it effectively. The Live Launch is a proven methodology that will enable you to achieve and enjoy six- and even seven-figure growth in your business is a strategic, sustainable way. The best part? It is easy, simple and fun.

First, everyone wants to know who the Live Launch Method is for and whether it will work for their business. The Live Launch Method is ideal for service-based business owners who want to leverage the power of social media and live video to sell online. We frequently share that the Live Launch Method is quite literally the simplest method on the planet to take prospects from cold to close in fewer than ten days and closing dozens of clients at once.

So to answer the question, "Will this work for me?" If you fall into this category and want the results I described above the answer is YES!

From those in digital media and marketing agencies to lawyers, doctors, financial planners and other professionals to consultants, speakers, and coaches, this method of growing any service-based business will absolutely work. Any type of service-based business (e.g., those that provide a transformational change for clients like those in the weight loss, fitness, and other wellness industries) can achieve incredible, scalable growth using the Live Launch Method.

Any type of business in which you provide a result for clients can benefit! If you are looking for scalable growth for your business, you've come to the right place – the Live Launch Method is the most powerful way to achieve this. You'll learn everything you need to know in this book to achieve your business goals – how you can bring your program, product, or service to the world in a meaningful way that will allow you to leap by six, multiple six, or even seven figures in your business simply and easily.

Before we delve into the nuts and bolts of the Live Launch Method, I encourage you to take the time you need with this book. Put aside other distractions and allow yourself to focus on what you're reading, so you can better apply it to your business. I know we're all busy. Every entrepreneur has a thousand ideas running through their head… and a thousand things on their to-do list. Try to put all that aside for a bit and place your focus on what you're about to learn. I assure you: You and your business will be well served by it because I know how it can result in incredible growth for you and ultimately lead you to an incredible life – one in which you scale and run your business in a way that doesn't allow your business to run you.

Give yourself the gift of being "present" in this book and the magical and exciting journey I'm about to share with you.

There are a lot of changes occurring in the world of online entrepreneurship, including being at peak market saturation with no indication that that's going to change.

We have moved into a new phase of consumers' approach to purchasing. Consumers want an "experience"; they want to know you and interact with you. They are 100 percent over the automation, the prefabricated content and the perfectly edited and curated photos. They want something so much better – they want human connection.

This is the best thing that could possibly happen for true thought leaders, visionaries and firebrands that want to create change and make a difference doing what they love.

As you will hear me say many times in this book: human connection is your super power. It's time to start a new conversation with your market and create an experience for them that they have never felt or experienced before.

That said, I know the Live Launch Method will help you be the disrupter in your market. Everyone is either going to be disrupted or be the disrupter. I want to help you achieve the latter and explode your business, offering something that none of your competitors can. The choice is yours right now: disrupt or be disrupted.

You need a superior strategy to stand out, differentiate yourself, and elevate your business so that you can place yourself into a category of one. I want you to be able to step into the next best level of you and be the disrupter in your market, so keep these words close to your heart: elevate, differentiate, and stand out! You will not believe how much your business and life can change by implementing the Live Launch Method.

Know Your Why

It's important to understand not only where you want your business to go in terms of growth but why. What is your big "why"? The big dream that you have… perhaps one that you consider at the start of each year as you are setting goals.

The dream may be to spend more time with your family, enable your spouse to retire, take your kids on wonderful vacations… even more than once a year. A new house. Saving for college tuitions. Saving for retirement. There is no right or wrong reason "why." Everyone's will be different and personal.

No matter what your big why is, it's time to get serious about determining what you need to do to make it happen. The good news is that I'm going to give you the road map on how to get where you want to go. And we're going to do it in a way that allows you to have both freedom and fun in your business.

You've already shown determination and have worked hard in your business. Now it's time to take all that hard work and determination and turn it into cold, hard cash that allows you to see a return on your efforts. If you're ready to get started like I am, let's jump in!

Why I Developed the Live Launch Method

When I started my own business in 2012, I found that I was searching and searching for the best way to bring my products and programs to the world in a meaningful way. I wanted to find a way to create the multiple-seven-figure business I run today that was the goal I'd set for myself. And I wanted to do it without working 20 or more hours every day of the week, with my business running me instead of the other way around. I worked really, really hard for many years and knew I deserved it. Honestly, I had a number of failed launches. I followed the product launch formula, I did webinars to create conversions, and I tried every method that was out there. What I discovered was that the antiquated, overly automated, pre-recorded, prefabricated, and (let's be honest) fake approach wasn't working for the average entrepreneur and certainly did not work for me. For most people, you will not get cold leads in a single-session webinar or pre-recorded video and have them convert into paying clients. I suspect that if you are working hard and trying those approaches, they're not working for you either, despite the brilliance of your program or product.

> *It all starts with making meaningful connections. Without those, you'll never get results.*

This is exactly why I developed the Live Launch Method! I wanted to connect with people in a meaningful way and be myself – it's a huge part of the success of my business, and I know you feel the same way. You want to be yourself and enjoy what you do. It's tough to enjoy the day when you have to pretend to be something you're not. More importantly, when you are not authentic, you cannot make meaningful connections. Without those connections, there can never be results.

I realized that all of the technology, moving pieces and expenses served as huge distractions and ultimately barriers to the sales.

When I started using the Live Launch Method, I began taking prospects from cold leads to paying customers in ten days. Yes, you read that right: cold to close in ten days. I've also had clients use the method and enjoy a $300,000 launch in the first month simply using what they learned and a smart phone. The most important thing about this method is to make it your own! It's designed to be flexible and dynamic, so it can work for any business in any industry and match you and your personality.

The Four Pillars

The Live Launch Method replaces everything you've ever learned about building, growing, and scaling your business and simplifies it to a content-to-conversion process. It takes all of the age-old and million-dollar strategies that every successful billion-dollar enterprise has ever used and brings those to social media. I've helped hundreds of entrepreneurs understand what their sales system needs to look like today and will help you learn how you need to show up online in the current market to produce six-figure and multiple-six-figure leaps in your business.

The Live Launch Method is extraordinarily effective because of its foundation – what I call the four pillars. They simplify the scaling process, so you can grow your business and run your business rather than your business running you and dictating every aspect of your life.

Pillar one is two-way engagement. The biggest issue in 2020 (as I write this) and beyond is the ability to scale intimacy. Technology advances have allowed everyone to be more connected than ever, yet almost everyone agrees that they actually feel more disconnected than ever. Customers and clients want their providers to bring the "real" back. They want to have a relationship with the person from whom they're buying, and they want to work with someone they feel they can connect and engage with. They want meaningful dialog more than an immediate autoresponder and pre-recorded video. They're actually 100 percent over and done with those things. They want something raw that's a new experience. They want to feel a person on the other end of the interaction they're having. No one wants to be a passenger on the "automated response train." They want to be a participant, working directly with the conductor, if you will. With pillar one, you create this two-way engagement your audience and prospects desperately want along with creating a live experience for them.

Pillar two is intuition – yours coupled with adaptability. You get to use your intuition and adaptability to drive the process every step of the way. You get to pay attention to the live interaction, so you can address what your prospects need from you. If you've tried other methods to promote and sell your programs, products, and services and felt like you were being shoved into something that didn't fit you, like a round peg in a square hole, I understand completely. That's how I felt with other methods… like I was being forced into something that did not fit me at all. The Live Launch Method is all about you connecting in an *authentic* way with the people you are designed to serve with your business. I want you to be yourself and have designed this method to allow you to do just that. You're going to take the principles that fit and put them to work for you, and you'll massage the model so that it fits your own personality and brand. The result is that you'll make meaningful connections with your prospects and customers who need the transformation you can offer them.

If you want to know why the other methods haven't worked for you, and probably won't ever work, it's because you have not had the freedom to be with the people you're here to serve – the freedom to be present with your audience. In the past and using antiquated methods, my team and I got so caught up in the technology, set up, landing pages, the hundreds of steps needed, and every other required resource that I couldn't focus on being present with my customers and serving them. Instead, we were caught up in video editing, creating slide decks, crafting web pages, writing email sequences… and that list went on and on – all things that were not central to serving and delivering on the promise. It was both exhausting and frustrating. Worst of all: it didn't work! There was no energy left for me to show up as my best self and provide the experience my prospects wanted and deserved. With the Live Launch Method, all you need is what I'm going to teach you and a smart phone. That's it. In a nutshell, that's pillar number three: the freedom to be present with your people, so you can create a human connection and break down the barriers that existed previously.

With pillar four, we're going to combine age-old sales and marketing strategies on which every billion-dollar company was ever built with the power of social media and livestreaming. We'll marry proven strategies and frameworks with simple technology, so you can deliver your message in an easy-to-consume, easy-to-access, and easy-to-interact format, and your market is absolutely going to fall in love with it. (I use my iPhone and the workbook I created. That's it.) They'll not only love you for it, they're going to decide to open their wallets and buy from you because of it.

Momentum and Motion

The Live Launch Method leverages two core power strategies that other launch methods simply cannot deliver. If you've been working hard, giving everything you have to selling what you have to offer and have not been able to generate positive results, I know for a fact that these two components have been missing.

First, when I teach you the Live Launch Method, you're going to learn how to create momentum and, second, how to help prospects take action so they get results while working with you for free that then demonstrate the incredible value you bring to the table. You set yourself apart, putting yourself in a class completely alone and making you the very obvious choice as the only one who can solve your prospects' problems with your program, product, or service. They will understand the value you deliver and will want to invest in it. Even those who don't opt to join your paid program will still be an ambassador for you because they've experienced the value you deliver.

No other program delivers on this law of leveraged momentum and velocity. Remember Newton's law: something in motion is likely to stay in motion. I'm going to teach you how to get your prospects and customers moving with this program! You'll get your people taking action... and continuing to take action. They'll first get results for free, and then (and here's the key), they'll want to *keep getting* those results, so they'll eagerly pull out their wallets and credit cards to continue working with you. They'll see the proof firsthand – the results they were able to generate before they ever started paying you!

With the Live Launch Method, you'll discover the process that can take weeks, months, or even years off the time needed for you to exponentially grow your business… to achieve exactly what you've been working so hard to create.

… And Mindset

To step fully into your purpose and own the space in your market and industry, you must have a million-dollar mindset. It's mindset before mechanics. It doesn't matter how well-perfected your mechanics may be. If your mindset is off, it won't matter and there is no way you will be able to achieve unstoppable success.

As we get into the Live Launch Method, you'll see that you'll want to fill your group with about 300 leads (minimum) to start and repeat the process and scale up from there. You do this six to eight times a year, and you will easily create hyper-scalable growth. That may sound daunting, but honestly, it all comes down to mindset. Most people work really, really hard at all the wrong things, and that is way more strenuous than focusing on the very few things that actually produce replicable, scalable results. Once you have dialed in your launch and achieved a baseline of revenue and profit you are happy with, you can slow it down and increase the time between launches, although by that point you probably won't want to because you will be having so much fun and making so much money!

Million-dollar, multi-million-dollar, and billion-dollar businesses all have at least one thing in common: **They are built, created, and sustained on an abundance mindset.**

This abundance mindset is going to give you the energy, passion, certainty, and drive you need to lead your company into a future of growth and prosperity. It's the same mindset that will enable you to fulfill your higher purpose... and the income and earning ability that come with that.

What is an abundance mindset? When it comes to lead generation (as we'll cover in a later chapter), consider that there are seven billion people on the planet, with at least a couple billion on social media! There are so many that it is actually impossible for you to meet the needs of all the people who actually want to pay you for your service. Ponder that for a moment. It points directly to abundance. You actually can't serve all the people who want what you offer.

When you understand this, you'll understand the opportunity that is available for you to build a multi-million-dollar business. Those who've built these businesses, myself included, understand that it's not about us. It's about being of service and filling a need that already exists.

Accept the fact that there are more people in your market than you will ever be able to serve and adopt that abundance mindset or you will struggle to be truly successful.

To share a personal story, I didn't start out as the self-made millionaire I am today. Actually, I grew up in a family with five kids and we struggled financially every day, with my parents always arguing about money. At month's end, there was no certainly that there was enough to cover the bills. When I'd finally saved up enough to buy my own car, the thing I most didn't want was a station wagon, a red one to be specific. I wasn't sure what I wanted, but I was completely sure about what I didn't want. With my $2,000 and parents' approval, lo and behold, the **only** car I could afford was a red station wagon.

It was my first and most powerful lesson about the power of an attraction mindset. I'd 100 percent attracted exactly what I didn't want because that's where my complete focus was. I learned how important it was to focus on what I did want and channel my energies toward that. The red station wagon lesson flipped the switch for me for the rest of my life to focus clearly on what I want and then attract what I want.

If you can focus energy the wrong way, getting what you don't want, you can also focus your energy the right way – on what you do want to attract it to you. When you do, your universe changes and your experience shifts. What you see and feel reflects back to you – either positive or negative. Make it positive!

Your mindset also drives your actions. The entrepreneurs who are most successful are like the most successful athletes who compete at the highest levels. They train and practice every single day. They execute on the same drills repeatedly, not once and done. Whimsical entrepreneurs try something once and then are quick to move onto the next thing. Whimsical entrepreneurs will never be as successful as they can be. Without training and the discipline to show up and take action every day, of course, they'll never reach their goals and realize their dreams. Success isn't magic; it's commitment. It's not magic; it's conviction. It's not magic; it's discipline, follow through, and focusing on your higher purpose. Commit to yourself to train like an athlete, so you can explode your business and live your dream. Commit to be the category of one that you know you can and deserve to be.

On top of that mindset, I want you to understand that all of those abundant prospects who want what you offer are also sick and tired of the plain vanilla solutions that everyone else, including your competitors, has been selling... or trying to sell. All of these prospects are waiting and hoping that someone like you will come into their world! They're looking for the pattern interrupt that you are ready to offer – something new, something different, something with the human touch that has been missing for so long.

They're looking for someone who is willing to go the extra mile. And I assure you: There's never a traffic jam on the extra mile. It's actually pretty empty, and your competitors aren't there.

Speaking of your competitors, I want you to ignore them. One of the best things I ever did was just that – ignore my competitors. I unsubscribed from their lists and stopped following them. Instead, I decided to listen to my own clients and prospects and innovate around what they wanted, focusing on what I did best and providing the human touch that was so sorely lacking.

I encourage you to do the same. Listen to your own intuition and follow your heart. Remember that intuition is one of the pillars of a successful live launch. Pay attention to what your gut is telling you and listen to your clients' needs. Put your energy there rather than worrying about what your competitors are doing. Once I did this, I blew every goal and expectation out of the water. You can do the same thing!

The 80/20 Rule

If you aren't familiar with the 80/20 rule, it's pretty simple: 80 percent of your results typically come from 20 percent of your effort. Stated another way, 80 percent of your revenue probably comes from 20 percent of your clients. Now let me turn that around and tell you that 80 percent of what you are doing right now is not affecting your bottom line. I could go into your calendar right now and delete 80 percent of the things you are doing and it would not impact your bank account. Crazy? Yes, but true, so it's time to change that.

The Live Launch Method can account for 80 percent of your company's growth and profitability, and you can implement this without really putting more time on your calendar. As you'll discover as we delve into the nuts and bolts of the program, you will set it up once and then "lather, rinse, and repeat."

You won't be working more hours in your business, but I do want to challenge you to step up and take the next step to eliminate those things that aren't getting you results and to delete from your calendar the 80 percent of the tasks that are completely ineffective. Instead, upgrade your activities, including implementing the Live Launch Method so that you're getting 80 percent of your great results from far less effort. Focus on what makes a substantial difference to your bottom line and, ultimately, the money you bring in for your family. The Live Launch Method will definitely make a difference and be worth your effort.

Having built my business while still working as an executive for a Fortune 500 and working 60-plus hours a week (and reaching multi-six figures ++ with my own business while doing so), I am all too familiar with the importance of focusing effort where you generate the best results. Again, that is exactly why I developed the Live Launch Method. If I can do it, I know you can do it too, so I'm giving you the upgraded megaphone you need to develop a superior system to work fewer hours while still producing greater results – more income and profitability.

Let's get started, so you can step into the true leadership position in which you know you belong. You've already been working hard to achieve this, and this system will be, I'm certain, the exact piece that's been missing. With this upgraded megaphone, your audience will better be able to see, feel, and hear what you have to share that is the solution that they need and the magic you have to offer.

Chapter One:

The Five-Day Content-to-Conversion Formula for Six- and Seven-Figure Breakthroughs

The Live Launch method is actually structured as an umbrella that encompasses various formats you can put to use to bring the greatness you have to offer to the world. To start, you'll begin with what I've created as the five-day approach. Once you have mastered that, you can begin to incorporate other formats, including the blitz method, the "live-inar" method, testing on different platforms, etc. Ultimately, the Live Launch Method isn't only about the five-day approach. It is a fixed, yet flexible, model that you can use in the format that works best and feels best for you and your business.

That said, the five-day approach can be likened to being your training wheels. You **always** want to start here and get really comfortable launching with this approach because it gives your prospects enough time to spend with you to move through the psychological buying process to bring them to "yes." In fact, I don't want you to change anything I'm teaching you about the five-day approach until you've done your first six-figure launch. Once you're doing six figures, you can get as creative as you want.

As the name says, with the five-day approach, you'll do a session every day for five days within your Facebook group. And yes, this really should be housed inside of a Facebook group. There are a hundred reasons I could cover regarding how you will generate more sales, more engagement, and overall better results in a group, but the two critical reasons are:

community and containment. When people are on a feed or page, they are easily distracted, scrolling through and looking at different things without being fully focused on your message. Additionally, there is a different sort of engagement on a public video than a private one. So work with the five-day format until you're getting six figures pretty regularly with each launch you do. It's the best way to move prospects from "cold to close" as you're refining your model or offer. I still love the five-day model and use it regularly.

The live launch is essentially a term for an umbrella strategy to help you understand how you can scale your business online using a content-to-conversion approach. The four teaching segments (i.e., the four pillars) are designed to lead participants to your paid program and give them a jump start to really get results. These will focus on the "must know" information, allowing the live launch to function as a serve-to-sell model.

To start, you'll design a "workshop." You can call it whatever you'd like, and we'll dive into naming later. It is essentially a free workshop, and for the first four days, you are going to put your whole heart into teaching… but teaching in a very structured way. You will address the number one thing you believe your prospects must know and get started on in order to set them up to move into your flagship program. The sessions you teach can run anywhere from 20 minutes to about an hour.

You'll break that topic into four pillars that will each be covered on sequential days and build the foundation. So, for example, pillar one on Monday, two on Tuesday, three on Wednesday, and four on Thursday. These are your four teaching segments as you roll out the five-day format. On day four, about halfway through your presentation, you are going to flip and extend the "invitation." This is when you'll create the opportunity for people who are very invested in what you're teaching and want to be a part of it. They've already gotten results and have completed the homework that accompanies the workshop. Your invitation gives them the opportunity to take the next step and bring the process full circle to get even greater results – actually working with you for a fee.

Again, the Live Launch Method is ideally designed for service providers, no matter what industry they serve – accountants, financial planners, doctors, attorneys, medical weight loss specialists, fitness gurus, consultants, speakers, etc. We've even worked with lawyers using the Live Launch Method successfully! Anyone who provides their customers with results and a transformation can successfully use this method. Additionally, you'll want to address an audience that's on Facebook. (If your audience isn't on Facebook, there is a hybrid method that I teach using LinkedIn, but the focus of this book [today] will be Facebook audiences.) And please keep in mind as you read this book… tactics change, platforms change, functionality changes. It's Facebook today, could be Instagram tomorrow and a platform neither of us have ever heard of next week. The key is to learn the skills, understand the methodology and start applying it.

The five-day approach works because you effectively elevate yourself into a category of one.

After the fourth day, you'll have five bonus days of selling: Friday through the following Tuesday. These sessions can be live Q&A sessions, client success stories and testimonials about your program or service, etc. The heart of the process is teaching and serving. It's most likely at the center of your own heart as to what you want to do for customers: teach and serve. By doing so, you elevate yourself and place yourself in a category of one, effectively eliminating your competition. You're going to lead your prospects to an unbelievable result (that we'll cover later in the book) for free. When you reach that and enter your bonus days, you're not even really selling. It becomes a complete no-brainer. Your prospects are already committed, having gained insights and results. Now, you are passing on additional certainty about future results and underscoring the message. You'll continue to provide them with exactly what they want.

So we say it's a "five-day workshop," but it actually encompasses ten days, which is why I say "cold to close in ten days." You can literally start with hundreds of people in the workshop who've never heard of you before, and by the time you get them to day ten (or sooner), they're going to be pulling out their credit cards, thrilled beyond belief to give you their money because of what you've just delivered.

This actually becomes your number one marketing tool, your number one visibility tool, and what you are known for in the marketplace that catapults you above the rest. It blows your competitors out of the water. Additionally, your workshop attendees become excellent referrals, encouraging others in their circles to participate as well because of the business- and even life-changing results they got! They spread the word for you and become your ambassadors. In fact, the Live Launch Method includes a "wow" factor that enables you to blow the socks off all of your attendees, making them want to shout about you – why they need to listen to you, why they need to follow you, and why they need to join your group and work with you. This becomes residual. Not only are you closing prospects during your live launch, you are always setting up the next group to participate.

It happened in my business, and I know this fantastic snowball effect can happen for your business as well. We already talked about momentum, and the snowball is a great metaphor. At the top of the hill, the snowball can start out very small, but as it starts rolling down, it picks up more snow and more momentum with every revolution. It's that law of motion in action.

You're the Expert

No matter where you might be in your business as you're reading this book – just starting out or already pulling down six or seven figures and wanting to explode it even higher – this is the best way to bring your program or service to the market. It allows you to truly position yourself as the expert you are and add revenue (even an additional seven figures) to your income stream.

You're continuing to teach through each session and building momentum, reciprocity, and rapport through your bonus sessions. The Live Launch Method allows you to serve at an extremely high level, so you can truly fulfill the purpose you are designed to live out in the most meaningful way every single day.

You'll also create assets in your business that you can repeat, saving you hundreds of hours of work. The inability to repeat and reuse assets is one of the main reasons so many entrepreneurs fail with their launches. They are always recreating the wheel. In fact, I suggest you create your first launch and then repeat that eight times in the first year. It is the ideal way to build your brand and elevate your business. Don't be surprised if prospects participate multiple times in your launches, and they will not be annoyed when you share the same content. Your audience is trying to learn from you – the expert, and that doesn't always happen the first time. I've even had some prospects participate six and seven times.

In fact, repetition is crucial. The more you repeat your live launch, the more you will be known in your industry and market as the expert, so the more you can elevate, differentiate, and disrupt what's happening in your market. Commit now to repeating the process, and again, you'll create your assets so that you can reuse them repeatedly. Do the work once and get paid for it over and over. What a relief that is!

Don't overlook your background and credentials that make you the one and only in your market. Consider three things about your experience that differentiate you from your competitors and make you uniquely positioned to deliver your solution… and then promote that. Never hesitate to position and promote yourself. They have to know why you are special and how you can help them. Scream from the rooftops that you're solving problems that no one else can. You're the expert. Let your prospects know that.

If you happen to be the entrepreneur who's just getting started, this method can be exactly what you need to generate your first paying client. The Live Launch Method doesn't rely on how long you've been in business or how many followers you currently have on Facebook or Instagram. Even if you are starting from zero, it's really a matter of filling your group with **qualified** leads.

I'll share my own quick case study: I had someone participate in one of my free five-day workshops who put what she'd learned into action and quickly made $20,000 within her first few days. She could see how by investing more, she could really up the ante on her own business and signed up for the paid program. This isn't an isolated incident; it happens all the time. You'll have the same thing in your business once you get this method rocking and rolling for you.

Whether you want to fill your calendar with private clients, fill an event, or build a membership group and max out your team members, the Live Launch Method will work for you by meeting you where you are and helping you to take the next step needed to achieve bigger and better results than you ever dreamed possible. I can state that unequivocally because I personally went from failed launch after failed launch to doing launches with ease by using this method… and those launches were, without exaggeration, $700,000 to $2 million and above! Plus, it wasn't simply the new revenue. I have had more fun and have enjoyed the process more every single step of the way.

You'll discover the same thing. Every time you conduct a launch, it gets easier and you have more fun. Absorb what I'm sharing and make a commitment to take action.

Getting Live Launch Results

- Using the five-day approach inside a Facebook group creates containment and community.
- Cover each of the four pillars that build the foundation on consecutive days, and then flip on Thursday and extend the invitation to join your paid program.

- Your prospects have already received your expertise and generated results for free, so they'll be ready to sign on during your five bonus days.
- Sharing your expertise for free puts you in a category of one, eliminating your competition.
- Create assets once and reuse them, so you are not always recreating the wheel, and don't be surprised if prospects participate in your live launch multiple times.
- Repetition is critical, and the more you repeat your live launch, the greater your credibility and ability to disrupt your market.

Ready to get your live launch on the calendar so you can add another six figures to your bottom line? Grab our free Definitive Live Launch Planner Guide here: www.kellyroachcoaching.com/livelaunchplanner

Chapter Two

Fill the Gap, Make a Fortune

By definition, a gap is an unfilled space, and the key word on which to focus is "unfilled."

Very few sales or business coaches address the concept of the gap, but I assure you, it's critical. I've been teaching it for years and have seen entrepreneurs generate unbelievable and mind-blowing success by employing this concept.

As we covered, you'll teach for four days and flip to the invitation in the middle of the fourth day, leading into five additional days of selling with bonuses and other informational sessions. During this time, attendees are signing up and raising their hands asking questions and declaring, "Yes! I'm ready to work with you and create a transformation! Here, take my credit card."

However, to achieve that reaction and response, you must sell to the gap. Selling to the gap is now critically important because of peak market saturation, especially in the online world. Most entrepreneurs think that they have the perfect program and… if people just knew about it, they'd sign on. They believe they simply need to get in front of more people, and when they do, they'll close sales like crazy and their revenue will skyrocket. Unfortunately, that is just not true. It's not the way it works.

Many programs are far too complex with too many fluffy adjectives and descriptors built in. Prospects cannot get a clear sense of what the program does. Additionally, many of these same entrepreneurs offer so many different programs, that prospects are completely confused about what the offer really is and, most importantly, what it will do for them. They don't know what or how to buy. I had the same problem, and in fact, it's exactly why I created the Live Launch Method in the first place – to use myself because there was no other solution. I didn't initially intend to teach it, but it was so successful for me that I knew I had to share it.

To avoid falling into this complexity trap, we're going to do some deep work in this book. I want you to simplify your program, product, or service down to "the gap." In every single industry, without exception, there is a gap. Let me repeat: There is always a gap. And that gap is the big missing piece that no one in your market has had the nerve, the guts, the patience, or the care and concern to address.

The gap is typically a matter of accessibility, human interaction, and accountability. Too many entrepreneurs became obsessed with "techno-touch" and focused on avoiding human interaction, hoping online tools would do all the work. The result was a move away from service. The truth is people will pay a premium to work with a provider who offers high-touch accessibility, human connection, and accountability! You can charge more without worrying about your competition.

> *Every industry has a gap. Find it and fill it.*

This is exactly why industry after industry… after industry is now being disrupted. These disruptions are occurring because innovative thinkers are starting to fill the gap! Start thinking now (and keep thinking as you read what follows) how you can fill the gap in your own industry. I assure you, a gap exists.

Let me use the Unstoppable Entrepreneur program as an example. About two years ago, we realized there was a major gap in the coaching industry. People were trying to consume information from a fire hose – never an effective way to learn. Entrepreneurs were going broke taking course after course and program after program trying all these different things, working their tails off trying to pull from all of the different things they'd learned – or thought they'd learned – from various gurus and mentors. After all these courses and mastermind groups, they were left **without results**. Why? Everyone in the coaching space became overly reliant and even obsessed with automation – tech without touch – trying to scale up with little to no actual interaction with people.

We decided to run as hard and fast in the opposite direction as humanly possible when developing our program. I hired an entire staff of accountability coaches who had no job other than to kick butts, push hard, stay in touch on a weekly basis, and make sure group members were taking action to actually generate the results they needed.

What happened? We turned this little program with a handful of participants into a multi-million-dollar program that is now known as best in class in the coaching industry. We're knocking down the competition and blowing them out of the water. How? We're willing to take the time and invest the energy and resources needed into accountability… accountability that only works with a human touch and does not rely on automation or technology.

Accountability is the critical difference between consuming information and taking action that produces income. It was the gap in our industry. We're invested right along with our clients, getting them to take action that produces results and revenue. We focused on building out the accountability coaching side of the business, and we became the first and only business incubator that is led by accountability coaching – the only one that places accountability at the top. By filling the gap, the results have been astounding.

Change Your Perspective

Get out of the bubble of your own expectations about what you're doing and what your competitors are doing and uncover the gap that, I assure you, exists.

Instead, turn it around and look at things from the perspective of your consumer or prospect:

- What is their experience like?
- What needs do they have that aren't being met?
- What are the things that everyone else in your market is failing to deliver?
- How are your prospects being disappointed, frustrated, and let down?

If you take the time to think about the answers to these questions, you'll likely uncover the gap in a matter of moments. Your existing clients and even some of your prospects have already shared the answers with you. Granted, they may not have articulated it directly, but they've probably shared it indirectly. You simply have to listen. "Oh, I'd love to have more of…." Or "I feel like I need more support on…." Or "What I really need is this, but I know that's not possible." These statements are allusions to what they really need and want, even if they are not able to state it outright or ask directly because it's not part of your current program.

A quick conversation with any prospect in your space will go a long way to revealing the gap. They'll share their issues in a matter of moments. With the Unstoppable Entrepreneur program, people constantly told us that they'd signed up for various programs only to discover there was no one accessible to them. Coaches were unavailable, and they couldn't get in touch with the person who sold them the program. Picking up the phone and talking to someone was impossible, and there was no one to whom they could shoot a quick text question. With that information and feedback, it was pretty easy for us to figure out how to fill the gap, and it won't be difficult for you to figure out how to fill the gap in your own space. Honestly, it only takes caring enough to do so.

When you care enough, you can fill the gap. There is only one super power needed, and you already have it: human connection.

Start now by taking a few moments to think about how you can step into the leadership role and place yourself in a category of one. Identify the gap and determine how you can fill it. Consider and answer the following:

What is the gap in your industry? _____

_____

Your Offer: _____

Your Ideal Buyer: _____

What do they want to accomplish? _____

_____

Why is it urgent? _____

_____

How can you simplify your offer? _____

_____

Take this important step that your competitors have been unwilling or unable to take, either because they didn't really care or didn't take the time to think outside the box. You'll become the one and only in your market. Before you go any further, you must ensure that your offer is ready and that it answers the need your prospects have and fills the gap that exists. Without zeroing in on your offer and ensuring it is complete and polished first, the best launch on the planet will not lead to success. By stating this by no means am I indicating that you need your program done or perfect. What I am saying is that it needs to be laser-beam focused on addressing the urgent need your market will pay you for now AND it needs to be obvious. (We'll show you how later in the book)

So when you solidify your offer and develop your five-day live launch, you'll do it with pride, certainty, and expertise that will flow through during your presentations. You'll be making sure that people truly understand that you are not a "me too" marketer, delivering exactly what they've already gotten too much of with disappointing results. Instead, you'll deliver a new and different alternative that provides your prospects with a superior experience that, in turn, generates the results they want and need but have never been able to achieve… before they met you.

Getting Live Launch Results

- Every industry has a gap: Find yours and fill it to be successful.

- Innovative thinkers are the ones disrupting industries because they are filling the gaps that exist.
- With the Unstoppable Entrepreneur program, we saw the gap in accountability, so we focused on providing that rather than relying on automation.
- Get out of the bubble of your own expectations and look at things from your prospects' and customers' perspectives.
- Listen to what prospects and customers are asking for or lamenting. That information is pointing directly toward the gap in your industry.

Step into the gap and launch your way to seven figures using our free Definitive Live Launch Planner Guide. Download a copy by visiting:

www.kellyroachcoaching.com/livelaunchplanner

Chapter Three

Fill Your Launch with the Best Caliber Leads on the Planet… and Quickly

There are plenty of technology expenses and frustrations that can play a part in any launch, and that's exactly why I created the Live Launch Method. I assure you, it doesn't have to be that complicated, and yes, it can even be simple and enjoyable to bring your program, product, or service to your prospects to achieve massive business growth. The best part is that it can be done by simply leveraging the power of your smart phone… from your home office, and even in yoga pants or whatever you choose to wear.

It doesn't matter if you're just starting out with little more than a business idea or if you already have a multi-million-dollar business and want to add another very profitable revenue stream. Live Launch Method success is not determined by how advanced your business may be. In fact, for those just starting, this is absolutely the best way to grow your business and grow it in a way that will continue to scale. Looking back, I'm sorry that I didn't have this method (and actually the technology wasn't there yet) when I started.

As you've already identified the gap in your respective industry, it's time to start filling your own live launch with prospects that you can take from cold to close in ten days or fewer. I'll caution you here that if you skipped over doing the "homework" in the previous chapter, you go back and do that now. You'll find I use a layered approach to building on the process, so you'll get the most out of it by completing the tasks I present in each chapter before proceeding.

In order to set yourself apart and stand out from the noise and clutter in the marketplace, you have to know how to sell to the gap. Again, the gap is that "white space" or open area in your market that no one else is addressing. As an example, if you're in the health and wellness space (e.g., nutrition, weight loss, etc.), the big gap is accountability. The same gap exists if you're in the coaching space. In real estate, the gap exists for sellers who have to continually leave their house for showings, and for buyers, it's having to drive around from house to house.

Regardless of your industry, the gap typically exists in the realm of accessibility, support through implementation, or convenience. Take a step back and look at your space through the eyes of a consumer, and one of those three areas is very likely going to pop out as the gap.

Urgency

I started my career in the Fortune 500 arena in sales, starting as a sales producer and moving into a sales leadership role, so I love teaching people how to sell. It's a passion for me. I love the thrill of the hunt, and I love the close. When I started my own business, I was excited to bring sales strategies to the market and teach entrepreneurs and small business owners how understanding sales and implementing that knowledge effectively would change their businesses and their lives, achieving financial freedom.

What I learned very quickly after some big ol' launch failures and flops in programs that focused on selling was that nobody wants to "sell." But... everyone wants to close clients, everyone wants to learn to be effective marketers to attract and magnetize the right clients. These out-of-the-blocks failures taught me the importance of addressing the urgent need that prospects wanted solved immediately and then giving them the tools and resources that I knew they'd need to succeed.

I did a quick pivot and focused on helping people learn how to market more effectively, position themselves correctly to attract top-tier clientele, and to handle client consultations in a way that converted. Take a page from my experience and pivot. Instead of selling what you're passionate about and what *you* think people need, redirect your efforts to selling them the urgent thing that they want. You can't sell what you're in love with. You have to sell to the urgent need of your prospects – what they're in love with. Take a hard look at your program, and if you aren't addressing what your prospects need and love, it's time to flip it around. Answer this question: What does your buyer want to accomplish and why is it urgent to them? This approach will be the difference between many failed program and product launches and many very, very successful ones!

In my case, I knew the market needed to understand how to sell, but that's not what they wanted, so it wasn't the right starting point. Take a moment to think about what your audience urgently wants and start there. Simplify your offer down to whatever the urgent want (and need) is. You never want your prospects to have to work to figure out what you do and how you can help them.

Instead, in a few words, make the value you deliver and what they're going to receive crystal clear to them. They have

> *Focus on the urgent thing that prospects want right now.*

to know exactly what the bottom line and end result will be… and it has to be something they urgently want. This approach will magnetize your prospects to you. Everyone is so busy, and no one has the time or wants to take the time to try to learn what you can do for them. Spell it out simply and succinctly. Hand it to them on a silver platter – exactly what you do and what they'll get.

Lead Logistics

You know what you want to sell, but the big question is always, "How do I generate the leads in order to close them?" We'll cover 12 ways you can generate ready-to-buy leads that can convert on the spot, so your live launch is a huge success and your revenue skyrockets. Are you ready to toss the over-complication, stress, anxiety, frustration, and wasted time and money caused by all the other mechanisms you've tried? Of course you are!

You have to know the math and have a plan to fill up your launch. I see way too many "silver-bullet" strategies being taught about how to grow a business without also providing the tools you need to generate the leads you need first! Without leads, you'll never hit the goals you set. It always starts with leads. You already have a goal for how much money you want to make and you know how many closes you need to hit that target. Now you need leads to generate that revenue.

Let's be clear about parameters for success. In live launches, of the people who put their hand up and register for the workshop, you're probably going to convert between two to five percent of those leads. However, I've had clients convert 40 (yes 4-0) percent of their attendees, so there's no reason you can't do that as well and crush that two to five percent figure. That said, let's stick with the two to five percent number for conversion.

To start, I don't want you to even worry about a registration page. Instead, simply send people to the Facebook group and start engaging with them, manually signing them up. Time spent with your people is time well spent... and better spent. Spend your time and energy interacting with your audience rather than focusing on and worrying about technology, landing pages, email sequences, and all those complicated tasks. Focus on simply spending time in your group and with your prospects.

> *Your goal: 300 leads to fill your group and a 2-5% close rate.*

As you interact with leads, you will want to gain permission to add them to your text message and email lists so that they never miss a valuable training or resource you release. We tend to gain these pieces of information in the entry questions to the group most of the time. Once you have your hands around the process and you up and running, then you can add in a landing page. Of course if you plan to generate leads with advertising, you will need a landing page right away.

With the two to five percent figure, you do not want to do a live launch without 300 people registered. For those of you who want to do six and seven figures out of the gate, you will need significantly more. That might sound like a lot, but I want to challenge your mindset about it. Remember the abundance factor and mindset that we covered in the introductory chapter and remind yourself that there are more people who want what you offer than you can possibly serve.

Also remember to focus on what you want, rather than on what you don't want, so you are attracting exactly what you want. Open your mind and heart and trust the process. Trust that the mechanisms and messaging strategy that I'm going to give you will allow you to get your 300 leads in a matter of days. I see people do it all… the… time! There's no reason you can do it as well.

These 300 leads must also be engaged, not just sitting in your group. Who you are being and how you are showing up determines the engagement of your prospects. If you want energetic leads, you have to show up with energy. Sit up, lean in, and believe in yourself! Who do you want to be? Who you are is who you'll attract as leads. Focus on attracting 300 (or 300 times 10!) of the type of prospects you want and that is what you'll get! Get over "scarcity thinking." ***Make your life your masterpiece!***

Take action to get them, no matter how imperfect that action may be. Imperfect action beats idleness every single time. The more action you take, the more money you make. Where there's a will, there's a way. Taking action and being disciplined leads to success every time. Action always trumps talent. Talent certainly matters, but unless it's matched with determination and the right mindset and energy, you'll never get the outcome you desire.

The WIN

With your 300 (or more) leads in place, the next step is to deliver the "WIN." Remember the law of momentum and motion that we covered at the start? Now is your moment to jumpstart this process and absolutely shock your audience with the incredible value you offer them for free. You want to get them moving and generating a result during your live launch right away. Once they get moving, they'll tend to stay in motion – motion that is the result of your expertise.

Everything about the Live Launch Method is about being of service. It's about impacting people to help them gain a new insight and new knowledge and to take a new action that will help them change their lives. You get to step into total authenticity, use your own intuition, and teach what it is that you know best.

We call it the WIN.

The W is Wonder and Awe. You've come to realize that through your program, product, or service, you can help people achieve a new result – a desired result and urgent want – that they couldn't before. And you'll generate hundreds of thousands of dollars in revenue by doing so from your home office using nothing more than a smart phone and a handout that you create as homework… simply by teaching what you know, providing a new insight to your prospects, so they get a new result.

The I is Instant Breakthrough. This is where the law of momentum and motion come into play. You get people to take a new action. During your live launch, you'll be assigning homework and asking attendees to take action that will create a breakthrough for themselves and generate results right now. And they're getting those results for free! With that, comes a sense of reciprocity as well as a bond with and trust in you. You become more than their mentor and guide by helping them achieve what they couldn't before. One of the best indicators of a successful live launch is getting comments like, "This is more valuable than the last two or three programs I *paid* for!" We get this feedback all the time. Focus on service and delivering so much value and simplifying how they can take action to get results, so they realize that you truly are the expert – the one and only! Teaching combined with caring makes all the difference in the world.

Finally, the N is the No-brainer Offer. How does it work and serve the client? Most marketers make it so difficult to figure out how to work with them and what value will be provided that prospects simply do not buy. When we work with clients in the Unstoppable Entrepreneur program, the first thing we do is review their social media and website, and all too often, we can't tell what they do or figure out what their offer is. Once we uncover the offer, it's often so complicated that we can't discern what result we'd get as a client. It's not clear why I should buy. In creating your no-brainer offer, simply and directly address what the urgent want is right now.

It's a WIN for your prospects, so it becomes a win for you as well. You deliver wonder and awe, an instant breakthrough through homework to take action, and a no-brainer offer that's so simple that it's crystal clear how and why to buy from you. Now you're the one and only, and your win is clients' reciprocity and a bond when they realize you care. Never underestimate the value of caring about your clients. It can literally be worth millions of dollars, and your competitors aren't doing it. Focus on caring, serving, and creating an authentic connection with people and the revenue and growth will take care of itself.

Filling Your Group

There are two primary approaches for filling your live launches and selling out your programs to scale and grow your business. First there is automation, and there is also the person-to-person "combat." Both work and both are equally important. The latter includes those personal actions that you take one by one that generate interest and get prospects registered… one by one. These absolutely work, and yes, despite the fact that the Unstoppable Entrepreneur program has grown so dramatically, I still use these approaches and will continue to use them, no matter how large the launch may be that I'm running. The flip side is automation, where you utilize paid traffic to scale up your registrations quickly.

The difference between these two approaches for filling your live launches comes down to spending money or spending time. In the person-to-person combat approach, you're investing your time without an actual cash outlay. Automation doesn't take time (or takes very little), but you must have the money to spend. Let me stress again that both of these are equivalent and both work, and I encourage you to take a hybrid approach.

> *Automation costs money. Organic costs time. Both work.*

Understandably, when you are starting out, you may not have the cash flow to drive paid traffic, and that's okay. Organic launches will work, and I still do organic launches as well and we can easily fill them through the person-to-person combat and contact, meaning we manually handle invitations. Even when you get to a point at which you have the funds to run Facebook ads, I encourage you to continue to utilize the person-to-person approach for invites because you don't want to become totally dependent on Facebook and its algorithms to determine who might see you and whether you'll be successful in filling your launch.

One of your first goals in doing a live launch is that you will raise the funds you need to hire someone to handle your social selling. Initially, you may have to handle everything; however, as your business grows, you will need to delegate more and more. You should be laser-beam focused on making that hire. Yes, it will mean paying someone else a salary, but it is beyond worth it! The increase you'll be able to generate in your sales, closes, and revenue becomes mind-blowing.

Here are 12 strategies to start filling your group to reach the 300 number:

Instagram Stories: Never underestimate the need to leverage all mechanisms on social media to get the word out about your programs, products, or services, including Instagram. We've sold countless program registrations and tickets through this social media platform. Also, never assume that just because you don't have high "engagement" on a piece of content that it's not working or that people aren't taking action. There have been plenty of times when I've posted a story or piece of content on Instagram that doesn't seem to be generating much only to have people message me through a different vehicle and comment on it saying, "I saw your post on Instagram and want to sign up," or "I saw something on Instagram and want to learn more about the Unstoppable Entrepreneur program." Don't get caught up in vanity metrics or worry about how many people are viewing. Be consistent. Engagement doesn't happen overnight, but with your consistency, it will happen.

Referral Giveaways: Honestly, I'm obsessed with these! No matter how big or small your group or client list may be right now, it's a group of people who know, like, and trust you. If they're attracted to your program, product, or service, it makes all the sense in the world that the people they know will want it as well. We asked people for referrals in a recent live launch and had over 100 referrals in a matter of minutes.

Get your group to help you continue to grow bigger and bigger, which in turn creates more momentum and greater opportunity. This is a great mechanism for person-to-person contact rather than sharing as a public post.

Your Personal Page: I am certain you are already connected to plenty of people who will be interested in what you have to offer. Extend the invitation. Share what you're doing on your personal page. Message your contacts: "Hey, not sure if you can use this, but maybe you know someone who can."

Instagram Feed: I already mentioned Instagram stories, which are ideal for quick engagement, but don't overlook the Instagram Feed, which is more evergreen and typically more planned. I've had many people make buying decisions driven by an Instagram post. In fact, we recently hired an Instagram sales rep to help us improve and really leverage this platform. We consistently add value there. People are converting based on this social media. Instagram cannot be overlooked, and despite my initial resistance to diving in, we had actual sales come in this way within 30 days of leaning in to use it the right way.

YouTube Teaser: Create a teaser that you can use at the beginning and/or end of your videos. It will allow you to get the word out, whether you have five, 500, or 5,000 YouTube subscribers. Use video to get the word out about your workshop! If you have access to the YouTube livestreaming feature, use it. Create a series of short, value-add videos on topics related to what you are going to teach and then have the call to action for each be your live launch workshop.

Email List: No matter how many – or more importantly how few – you may have on your list, get your message out! Contacts are on your list because they've already taken a step to show interest in you and what value you can provide to them. Keep sparking that interest! It is so important to respect every single person who's given you the gift of their attention. These days, we live in a world in which too many entrepreneurs are obsessed with volume over personal contact and service. Be grateful for every person who has engaged. Every lead matters in your ability to reach your goals. Each live launch workshop you run you should be sending a minimum of three to five emails to your list inviting them to attend. Remember that your raving fans and best clients will go through your sessions five, six, maybe even more times.

Facebook Messaging: If you already have a group, be sure that you or someone on your team is connecting with and friending the people in your group to pull them into conversations. Too many times we see the focus solely on getting people into the group but then failing to engage with them at all. They're not messaging them or chatting with them. The result is a group filled with a random collection of people who don't really know you at all. Group members bounce in and then bounce out just as quickly. It helps no one. Engage them one by one and nurture the group with consistent value-add resources on a consistent schedule and rotation.

Instagram Messaging: We live in a very magical moment in all of history to have the privilege and opportunity to use a smart phone to hand select the exact people with whom we want to work. The fact that we can send private messages or live stream is amazing! It is a wonderful opportunity to have these tools at our fingertips. It's up to you to be grateful for the magic of being able to use these tools and leverage their full effect in your business. With Instagram messaging, you can select the followers you already have or the followers *you want to have.* Begin engaging on their content and follow them. Typically, that's a reciprocal action, and they convert to become your group members and ultimately your clients.

Client Ambassadors: We have Unstoppable Entrepreneur influencers who introduce us to other entrepreneurs who they think will benefit from either the Unstoppable Entrepreneur program or the Live Launch Method workshop. We get hundreds of new registrants as a result of others introducing us. Creating an ambassador program is an easy, low cost way to be consistently getting introductions to others who want and need what you offer.

Podcast Guest Appearances: Since about 2014, I've been featured on one to two podcasts every week. It's been a huge part of my own marketing strategy. Not only do we have a top-100 podcast, we've been able to build it by participating on other podcasts. Get out there and start getting onto other podcasts as a guest. We get countless people who either join the Tribe of Unstoppables or attend a live launch because they found out about us through a podcast interview. This is both a short- and long-term strategy for growing your business.

Livestreaming: You can live stream on Instagram, YouTube, Facebook, LinkedIn… do so everywhere you possibly can. This is your megaphone to the world to let people know about your expertise and everything you can offer. "I am here to help you achieve the results you want that have eluded you to this point! Here's the workshop I offer and here's exactly what you can get out of it." It doesn't need to be scary and it will get easier with practice. You can set up a private group and practice livestreaming in it, so no one outside that group can see or hear anything you're doing. Start by thinking about one thing you want to share or teach. Live streams don't need to be long. In fact, often, shorter is better.

Facebook Stories: Make sure you are also pushing "stories." Some social media pundits believe that the transition from feeds to stories is the future of Facebook. The story is a temporary post that may be gone in 24 hours, but it may be seen by more of your followers than a news feed post. Another benefit is that when someone views your story, you can check who's viewed it. With a post, you're reliant on comments and likes to gather those analytics.

Finally, be on the lookout for cooperative ventures like joint video exchanges with other entrepreneurs in which you can share information with their audiences and vice versa. I do them on both Instagram and Facebook, bringing in someone as a guest and then appearing as a guest on their video. I invite them to share their group and whatever they have to offer that I believe will be valuable to my people, and then I share the Tribe of Unstoppables.

These are all incredibly powerful tools for you to put to use now to market your business and promote your live launches, bringing in high-quality leads – people who are intentionally raising their hands and asking for what you have to offer. "I want to learn what you're teaching. I want the solution that you provide!" Generating quality leads enhances your ability to take prospects from "cold to close" quickly.

Be specific in what you offer to keep lead quality high. When it comes to generating leads, quality trumps quantity every time. Ten high-quality leads who are very interested in what you offer and of which you have a great chance to close and convert them into a client is better than 100 ho-hum leads that may or may not be interested in your program, product, or service.

Using even one of the mechanisms I've shared in this chapter will get you on your way to generating quality leads and moving your business forward. I recommend you choose the ones that best fit your style and work for you and use them in combination to reach that 300 live launch registrant goal. Employ them all, as I do, and the sky's the limit. Keep that abundance mindset in the forefront of your brain! The only thing standing in the way of your ability to generate 300 leads is your own mindset. Remember, there are more prospects who want what you offer than you could possibly serve.

Outbound Messaging

Your focus from the standpoint of outbound messaging should be Instagram and Facebook. (Most people who are strictly on LinkedIn will not likely switch platforms and engage on Facebook.) Your goal is to develop a really simple outbound message that goes something like this:

Hey <insert name>: We're connected here on Facebook and I noticed that it looks like you're into <a,b,c or x,y,z> or it looks like your business focuses on <topic>. I want to let you know that I help people to <insert your value offering and the delivered result> with my <program, product, or service>. I'm offering a free workshop in a few days during which I'll teach you <this, this, this>, and I'd love for you to join the party, so please consider this your personal invitation. If this happens to not be entirely relevant for you, you can certainly ignore this message; however, if you happen to know someone who would benefit and be a fit, I'd love to have you extend this invitation on my behalf. Does this sound interesting to you?

It's very short, but it is a power statement in which you share the results you'll help people achieve along with an itemization of what you are going to cover and what they'll learn. It ends with a direct question about their interest.

You'll find that people are much more likely to respond and engage with you… and join your group… when you are inviting them to something specific. There's a timeline and a deadline along with specifics, and prospects appreciate that. Even if they reply with a negative, it opens the door for you to easily and politely inquire about anyone else they might know who would be interested.

Craft your outbound messaging right now:

Headline: _____

Your power statement about the results you'll deliver:

_____

_____

Three things attendees will learn:

1) _____

2) _____

3) _____

Invitation to join: _____

Plus, you'll use this same message in all of the mechanisms we covered. You don't have to re-invent the wheel each time. This is how simple it is to generate leads and ultimately six figures of income with outbound messaging!

Getting Live Launch Results

- Don't focus on selling what you're in love with… focus on the urgent thing your prospects want and need right now.
- Nothing happens without leads.
- The typical close rate is two to five percent, but it can go as high as 40 percent.

- Your goal for a live launch should be 300 registrants minimum for the first round, and then you can scale up from there.
- Remember the WIN: Wonder and awe, instant breakthrough, no-brainer offer.
- Use a combination of the various mechanisms to fill your group. Choose the ones that fit you and be consistent!
- Create your simple yet powerful outbound message.

It's time to start bringing in those leads in preparation for your first six-figure live launch. Before you get started, be sure to download our free Live Launch Planner Guide to set yourself up for six-figure success! www.kellyroachcoaching.com/livelaunchplanner

Chapter Four:

The Time Is NOW for Your Million-Dollar Breakthrough

With the Live Launch Method, one of the benefits is that it is like a spigot you can turn on any time to generate sales, and you know where those sales will be coming from. It will truly become a million-dollar asset in your business, leading you to double, triple, or quadruple your revenue and achieve financial freedom.

Having done the work in the previous chapter and employing any or all of the mechanisms I shared to fill your group, you are now on your way to generating the leads you need. Plus, the days of having complexity, automation, or any barriers come between you and those important leads are over! Instead, simplicity is everything. It is the cornerstone of the Unstoppable Entrepreneur program. My genius is helping other entrepreneurs simplify their paths to success. I want to do the same thing for you, so it's time to really bring your own live launch to life!

Your live launch is your number one brand-building asset. For years, as a business coach, I've helped countless entrepreneurs grow their businesses, even before creating the Live Launch Method. However, once that was implemented, it helped my own business skyrocket to become one of the leading coaching companies in the country. So I know it works because I've experienced it firsthand. Our reputation began preceding us, and we'd get referrals from referrals who had gone through the training. Comments like: "It's the best training I've ever done." "I got so much value out of it." "My results are amazing."

New prospects come into the group who were actually sold by someone else… not by me and not by anyone on my team. They're hearing from others that they have to join and participate because it's life changing. So your live launch is not only your best-selling tool, it is the single asset that will catapult the growth of your business for years.

That said, I'll be honest. As I write this, there's likely a recession or at least an economic downturn on the horizon. Why do I say that? We've been enjoying a real boon, but the economy always grows and retracts. It's always a roller coaster ride. When it goes up, it invariably has to go down again at some point. History bears that out.

Secondly, technology is always changing and changing faster every year. Just a few years ago, the Live Launch Method wasn't possible because the technology wasn't there. I can't predict when, where, or how technology will change again in the future, and those potential changes may reduce the effectiveness of a live launch. What I do know is that it's working – and working really well – right now, and there is no market saturation at this point.

What I also know is that you can easily deliver the same live launch six or eight times in the coming year, and by doing so, it is not unthinkable (and certainly not impossible) to add a million dollars to your revenue. In fact, you should be

> *Success is always the result of implemention and action. It's never created by information alone.*

doing live launches six to eight times a year. Using this strategy you will be able to put your family first, achieve financial freedom, and have the time to take care of your own mental and physical health. I can state that because I'm living proof. I developed the program because I was embarrassed and even mortified by all of my previous launch failures – webinars, sideways sales letter, the PLF (product launch formula) method, and every other one that was out there… and I failed, and I failed big. The Live Launch Method changed it, and now I'm enjoying million- and multi-million-dollar launches, business success, and financial freedom, and that's not limited to me or a select few entrepreneurs. It is available to anyone who uses the program, follows the steps, and takes action!

Provide a Jump Start

To start, you should be live launching your flagship program. It is the program on which you spend 80 percent of your time and expend 80 percent of your energy. Yes, you can be selling other programs and products behind the scenes, but your outward facing launch is one thing and one thing only.

In taking any prospect through your live launch, you should be focused on helping them get a jump start, so that when they move into your paid program, they're already ahead of the game. I've found that when prospects go through our live launch and then become clients in our program, within 30 days, they've already recouped their entire investment in the program.

Again, it focuses on service. Your goal with your live launch is to help people get a "wow" result. (Remember the WIN: wonder and awe, instant breakthrough, no-brainer offer.) The live launch should be giving people a huge advantage, so they're ten steps or more ahead of everyone else and able to more quickly achieve that first important milestone of outcomes almost immediately upon joining your program as a paid client.

Your live launch should be positioned to feed directly into your program. Positioned that way, you must determine what work your participants will do in your live launch workshop that will continue to benefit them in your paid program. What you cover in your live launch should provide participants with a head start for what you'll teach in your program. You want to enable them to get those immediate results! You want them to declare that it's the best investment they ever made. Essentially, your live launch is a teaser of all the great things they're going to receive and get out of your program.

You may not currently have something designed at the start of your program that's a "quick start" or "fast track." This is important because everyone has such short attention spans these days. Take time to re-evaluate your offering, and if you don't already have some sort of "mini course" or element that provides your client with an almost immediate ROI, you'll want to add that. Then your live launch literally moves them right into this.

Here's an example from my own business: For a long time (feels like forever), I struggled to sell the Unstoppable Entrepreneur program because it is a huge, comprehensive business incubator. I teach clients all of the billion-dollar corporate strategies that I've learned throughout my career in the Fortune 500 world, covering sales, marketing, team building, positioning, and more. It's a full curriculum that examines infrastructure, lead generation, sales and marketing, team building, and finance – every single thing that goes into building a company. And I was trying to sell that… but it's too much and too complex to "sell." Prospects and clients become overwhelmed and get confused. There is no *immediate* win or successful milestone achieved. I was too focused on the huge big picture rather than the urgent need.

So I created a "quick start" that is positioned at the front of the Unstoppable Entrepreneur program. In this quick start, we sell and teach the back end system of our proprietary sales strategies and the design of the five days of selling at the end of our live launch. Anyone who participates in the live launch now has a jump start on the program.

We know that ultimately people want to build a great business and an awesome team and have a company that will support them and enable them to achieve their goals. But the urgent desire is to grow income… immediately. The Live Launch Method is now the first thing we cover in the paid program, and those who come into the program having gone through our own live launch are way ahead of the curve coming in.

> *Sell them what they need right now… then give them everything else they need.*

Your own live launch has to sell a similar immediate tactical breakthrough and result that you can generate for your prospects and clients. This is a much more effective approach than attempting to explain and sell them on *everything* you are going to teach. Trying to do that simply doesn't work. People need something very specific that they can grasp immediately.

Super Short

It's time to simplify and get rid of all of the fluff and extra description that you may have been told you have to use in promoting your program, product, or service. For your live launch, I want you to develop a very focused, short title. And when I say "short," I mean it: four words or fewer. It should give a mega-specific focus on the result you will produce for your participants.

You want prospects to clearly understand in the first few seconds what they are going to learn in your live launch, whether that promotion is through an Instagram story or short Facebook Live segment. You want to address their urgent want so they can see themselves and say, "That is me... and I want it right now." A confused mind always says, "no." Your goal is to communicate in three to five seconds exactly what you are going to teach and the result participants will get immediately. Commit now to simplification.

Here are some examples of past live launch titles that we've used... and they all work:

- The Live Launch Workshop
- Side Hustle Launchpad
- Online Visibility Bootcamp
- Write Your Book, Scale Your Business Intensive
- Profit Lab
- Launch Lab

Words like master class, bootcamp, intensive, lab, launchpad, workshop, mini course are all powerful descriptors. Plus they all immediately convey the concept of action. To develop your title, take what you are going to teach and add one of these words at the end, and voila, you have the name of your live launch.

Other examples:

- Menopause No More Workshop
- Get Paid to Podcast Launchpad
- Franchise Profit Secrets Intensive
- Real Estate Profit Masterclass
- Postpartum Fitness Bootcamp

No matter what industry you serve, this works. You want it to be "on the nose" – no-brainer obvious. There are other times when a more nuanced or creative approach is warranted, but "this ain't it." You absolutely want "on the nose." Get rid of any adjectives and fluff words. Simple. Obvious. That's where the power is. Extra words and over explaining give your power away. Here are some key title considerations:

1. Does it scream an obvious end result?
2. Does it simply address an urgent problem right now?
3. Does it deliver in three to eight seconds exactly what they'll get out of it?

Time to name your live launch. Don't obsess and over think it. Remember: simplicity rocks and you have about three seconds to grab attention.

My title: _____ _____ _____ _____

Ultimately, your live launch is all about you getting re-connected with your purpose and why you began your business. You have a purpose for being on the planet and there's a reason why you're here. That reason involves serving and your ability to make a huge difference for a big audience. The Live Launch Method simply gives you the keys to the kingdom to unlock your potential… but you must take action.

Getting Live Launch Results

- Simplicity is key; it removes any barriers between you and your prospects.
- The Live Launch Method is wildly effective right now. That may or may not change with technology, so get started now and plan six to eight launches for the next 12 months!
- Your live launch should provide a jump start, so participants hit the ground running when they join your paid program.
- Your paid program must have a "quick start" or "fast track" positioned at the beginning, so your customers get results and an immediate ROI.
- Title your workshop in four words and use one of the powerful, proven descriptors.

Map out your first live launch with our free Definitive Live Launch Planner Guide, so you can live out your purpose while building your multi-million-dollar empire.

www.kellyroachcoaching.com/livelaunchplanner

Chapter Five

The Content-to-Conversion Method That DOES THE SELLING FOR YOU!

In order to utilize the Live Launch Method to convert the wonderful information that you're teaching into money in your bank account, you must make a smooth transition from your content into the conversion process. Of course, you want leads and live launch attendees and participants to become paying clients.

Is it worth it? Yes! The Live Launch Method is far easier than scraping by, trying to claw your way to getting a single client at a time. You know that you cannot grow your business or even keep it afloat by closing only a customer a week. Instead, you can close hundreds of clients in ten days or fewer! Again, let me repeat: ***The Live Launch Method is the number one strategy on the planet to take prospects from cold to close in ten days… or fewer.*** When you put this into action, you'll realize that you've turned a corner in your business and your life, and you will never look back.

You'll be able to unlock unlimited potential to be the leader you've been working so hard to be. I hear so often from entrepreneurs that they're continually taking massive action, yet that action never translates to dollars in the bank. The Live Launch Method changes that!

You've probably done months and months or years and years of work already developing and executing your program, product, or service. This strategy acts like the zipper that pulls all that together and creates a perfect culmination of it. It provides a new methodology to connect in a different – and personal – way with the people you want to serve without all the technology headaches and huge expenses that other methods create and require. Yes, there are a lot of megaphones you can use, but this one works. Many of the others set you up for failure. Technology and expense create barriers between you and your audience. Let's remove them!

Pulling the Power Levers

As we covered in the previous chapter, you want to teach and provide your live launch attendees with what they need to know to really get a head start once they're in your paid program.

In terms of conversion, the first and most important factor – or power lever to pull – in the Live Launch Method is scalable intimacy. I call it a "fixed yet flexible" model because you can use your intuition, make changes as you go, meet your audience where they are, and interact with them in real time. It is critically important for you to connect with the people you're serving and have the chance to learn and understand their needs. This is why you house your live launch inside a Facebook group. You can really get to know your prospects who are going through your live launch in ten days, paying attention to their comments and questions. There is gold in the posted comments and posed questions. They indicate what your clients need from you, so they can successfully take the next step they need to take.

So the first power lever you want to pull in your live launch is to use scalable intimacy to create true connection with your group. You'll do this long before you get into the actual sales process so that when you're there, you are already engaging with prospects and they're starting to really know, like, and trust you.

The second lever: Make sure you are messaging and chatting with people pre-launch. You cannot wait until the end of the process. As people start joining your group, you want to immediately begin building rapport with them, and you can't do that if *you* aren't engaged and building a relationship with them. It could be you or someone on your team messaging and chatting, but it's all about connection and human interaction. You want to leverage the human touch because any type of automation will never be able to generate the same results – the results you want. The human touch is a super power when it comes to conversion.

The third lever to pull during your launch is tagging. A lot of clients are very nervous about tagging because they're afraid of how those in their group will respond to it. I assure you: We get so many thank-yous

Make it easy for people to buy from you!

and positive comments when we tag people because there is so much happening so fast that it enables them to more quickly find what they're looking for. Your job in conversion is to make it easy for people to buy from you!

They can't or won't buy from you if they can't consume the information in your videos, and they can't consume the information if they can't find the videos. It's a preconceived notion to think that your prospects will be annoyed or frustrated by you tagging them. Wrong! They'll fully appreciate it because you are making it easy for them to engage with you, find the content, consume the content, and ultimately say "yes" to take the next step.

There are other tactics to use in conjunction with your tagging lever. Use the Facebook group units. This is another way to make things easy for your attendees. They never have to leave the group. Units will help you organize your information and content, and when it's organized, it's easy for your group members to find and review.

Also, use reminders! Everyone is busy. Remember that eight-second attention span. Your people will be happier to get multiple reminders than annoyed by them. Remind, remind, and remind again. Remind about the schedule, when you're going live, and what topics you're covering. Send emails with the information, post in the group, create an event for each live session. Do everything you can to make it *easy* for them to show up and participate!

Use the group banner to post the schedule for your launch. We post the initial schedule and then flip it after the invitation, and this works beautifully. You want to be accommodating and serve your audience. The banner is the immediate "go-to" spot and couldn't be more obvious. Make it easy to find and you make it easier to learn. Make it easy to learn and you make it easier for people to take action. Make it easy to take action and you're on your way to making the conversion easy.

Also use replays between live sessions. Not everyone will be in your particular time zone, so you don't want to exclude them because your live time may not be conducive to their schedule. Post visual recaps as well. They are game-changers.

The Live Launch Method works beautifully… as long as people watch the videos, so you must make them easy to access! You must remind about watching them. If your prospects don't consume your videos, they'll never become clients. There is a true connection between these tactical approaches and having any prospect take the final step and join your paid program.

The fourth power lever is to provide a free result that is superior to the last three things they paid for. Make a promise to yourself to achieve this. How? Make it simple, make it simple, make it simple. When creating the pillars in your program, ensure that they're progressive and building on one another. As you'll recall, I already had you create a title that was four words and "on the nose." Homework and assignments must be things they can do and implement immediately. You want them to see progress and get excited about it to keep the momentum going and growing.

Your fifth and final power lever is the homework. For the Unstoppable Entrepreneur program, in the business space, "homework" makes sense for that audience. However, in my Give Her Courage business, it doesn't make sense for me to assign "homework" to the moms who participate. They're tired of already doing homework with their daughters after school. Instead, we give "courage actions" for them to take – something to help them build community. Think about your own business and industry. What is an action you can encourage your group members to take? If it makes sense to do it in a "homework" setting, that's fine. If it doesn't match your particular space, do something different, but keep in mind the goal: getting them to take a new action that will get them results. The key is getting your prospects a result… and a WIN.

You will employ these levers from the time someone joins your group until your live launch, whether it's the content or sales stage.

As you'll recall when we covered the five-day approach, day four is when it's time to transition into your offer. You've explained your important four pillars, so your participants have what they need to get started. "Congratulations! You now understand the most important pieces of the puzzle, so you can jump in and get started. You are ready to go out into the world and execute for the results you want. But if you're not 100 percent sure that you can get the big outcome that you really want, stick with me because I'll be introducing something that will make a world of difference."

With this said, you can transition right into introducing your offer. It's very natural and smooth. For those who are confident to move on alone, you've offered your congratulations and have thanked them for all the work they've done and for their time and participation, but for the majority, you're enticing them that there is more to come.

Mapping Your Live Launch Dates

It's time to make it real by determining your live launch date. That creates the deadline for the rest of the structure you need and how you can work it on your calendar. Now we can get really excited about how all of your goals, dreams, and everything on which you've been taking action is going to come to fruition.

You'll start with a promotion period and group building. Remember that you'll want a minimum of 300 registrants to join, and I recommend giving yourself a minimum three weeks to achieve that target. During the third week, you'll offer your pre-launch content and really getting people stoked about the workshop.

Determine your live dates. I recommend kicking off on a Monday, and you'll run Monday through the following Tuesday. Again, for the first four days, you'll be covering your four pillars – one on each day, building on the previous. If your audience is very active during the weekend, you can certainly use that time in your launch, or you can stick to weekdays if that is when your group is most active and engaged.

You'll open the shopping cart on the fourth day (typically Thursday) once you flip from teaching content to extending the invitation. The "open cart" runs for, more or less, five business days. I don't recommend that you extend beyond six days. Spend this time and perhaps the following week gearing everyone up for the program start date. It is ideal to create your flagship program in such a way that you can run it, start to finish, in about six weeks, keeping it evergreen. Then you can cycle through the process again, so you have big groups of customers continually coming in while it's also customized for those who've been in the group, so they're getting that important human connection and level of support they need. The evergreen approach allows you to continually bring new customers in rather than having to start and stop.

Your schedule in a nutshell:

- Three weeks of buildup, with the last week used for your big excitement building, so your participants are really fired up.
- Content week of the actual live launch.
- Flip on the fourth day and spend four to six days in open cart. During this time, you want to block out your days to have time available for consultations and one-on-one contacts to close your prospects.

- During the back end of the week following live content and teaching, you'll be getting everyone set up for success.
- Program starts!

You are now ready to commit to a date on your calendar!

Pre-challenge Action Steps

Your success on the back end of your launch depends on the steps you take on the front end of it. What you do pre-launch and pre-open cart determines your results. This is also why you need to employ the power levers we covered earlier in this chapter. You have to be turning up the excitement the whole time, not just during your open cart phase. That way, you're continuing to nurture them and move them through your sales funnel and logical buying process. When you do, by the time you get to open cart, your prospects are thinking, "Hell yes. I'm all in!"

You must have a custom, human connection from the moment they join your group. Again, it's about scaling intimacy that we covered at the start. Focus on this! While your competitors are automating and digitizing, you're being human. You're focusing on your super power: human connection. Honestly, if you are struggling to determine the gap in your industry, I can tell you what it is without even knowing your space – it's human connection and touch… someone who cares.

Next, you'll need give-away bonuses. These help build the anticipation and excitement. Think about the give-away bonuses you can offer that will help your group get excited about what they're about to learn but will also integrate with your program.

Create the experience you want your participants to have. We hear from people all the time about how the Unstoppable Entrepreneur group is so extraordinarily special. We know it because we created and designed it to be exactly that. The energy, excitement, passion, and power that members feel is completely intentional. We literally sit around a table in our meetings and discuss how we are going to create the experience we want members to have. The experience and the connection matter, so be certain what happens during your launch is by design. Decide what *you* want the experience to be for your group. If it's not what you want, it will never be authentic. In doing so, you'll capture the energetic alignment that takes the content you teach and fuses it with passion that translates into dollars in your bank account.

Use real-life conversations to dial in your message. For example, before I go live, my team messages me with information about what the group needs help with and their comments. "Make sure you touch on this; don't forget to talk about that." You don't need a team to help, especially when you're getting started. Simply scan the feed for comments and check messages to start interacting.

Getting Live Launch Results

- You can't survive closing a customer a week. The Live Launch Method helps you close many in ten days or fewer.
- Employ the power levers to make your live launch successful:
  - Scalable intimacy

- o Pre-launch messaging and chatting
- o Tagging, plus using Facebook units, reminders, and replays
- o Provide a free result
- o Homework

- Map your live launch dates with a promotional period (three weeks prior), live launch week (starting on Monday), open cart period (typically the fourth day of the launch, running for five to six business days), and finally, the program start date.

- Take the right actions before your live launch and conversions will be easy. Include human connection, give-away bonuses, real-life conversations.

Use our free downloadable Definitive Live Launch Planner Guide to map out your pre-, during, post-launch plan, so you can show up, be present, and serve your prospects with absolute focus.

www.kellyroachcoaching.com/livelaunchplanner

Chapter Six

Live Launch Logistics

The live launch is about helping you reconnect with the reason why you went into business in the first place. As you create a magical, fun and supportive environment for the people you are here to serve, you begin to feel and see and understand your calling as an entrepreneur more deeply. You can actually see and feel people changing, learning and growing in your presence. It is truly life changing.

Make your impact in the world and be of service to your prospects and customers. Why were you put on the planet and who were you put here to serve? How can you step into your full leadership role to help your customers achieve the transformation they desire? Provide results and encourage action. This is the premise on which the Live Launch Method is built – creating something amazing for free. Taking the next step, investing with you, is then so obvious. Keep the WIN at the forefront: wonder and awe, instant breakthrough, no-brainer offer.

Focus on building real relationships in the chat. Our group members constantly comment about the unbelievable level of support they get from us. It makes a huge difference, so be certain you are replicating that as well. Questions are answered, engagement occurs daily, and there is plenty of interaction. These are all components to building relationships that then continue seamlessly in the paid program.

Likewise, engage in the feed. Offer congratulations on successes, answer questions, encourage action, and continue the human touch point. You take on the role of teacher, guide, and cheerleader for your group. It's what make the whole experience so powerful. Remember: human connection is your super power!

In getting into some of the logistics of the Live Launch Method, I recommend that your livestreams last from 20 to 45 minutes. Sometimes, they'll approach one hour depending on the level of engagement and also the space in which you operate your business. If you are teaching more in-depth topics and strategies, your sessions will be closer to 45 minutes than 20 minutes. Use your judgment about the length.

Remember the law of motion that we covered at the start: an object in motion is likely to stay in motion. You can keep the motion going with your homework offering (or named something else if that makes sense for you) to keep your audience engaged and focused. Engagement leads to conversions and sales. Get people to take action and create a breakthrough, and you'll get people to open their wallets and sign on with your program. Keep your action steps simple and manageable to keep the motion going and the momentum building. Your prospects have to put one foot in front of the other to get their results. Taking imperfect action is always, always better than taking no action at all.

Take a moment now to determine what your homework or imperfect action steps will be:

_____

_____

_____

_____

Engagement is critical. If people don't tune in for your livestreams or watch the videos later, they are never going to buy. Focus your energy on ways to keep your audience engaged content. Here are three approaches you can use for engagement:

1. Create "catch-up" plans in which you tag people to help them through the process. No matter when you plan your livestreams, there will always be people for whom the time doesn't work or who have something come up that precludes them from participating while you're live.
2. Homework is a huge factor in getting participants to take action.
3. Finally reward them with incentives and giveaways for those who do complete the homework and take their action steps. It also keeps it fun for everyone involved.

Never think that simply because someone is behind or not participating during the livestreams that they are not a viable prospect. I've had a number of people who come in at the end having binge watched all the videos and sign up. However, it's up to you to keep reaching out during your launch and extending the invitation to participate. You can also promote "watch parties" to help people catch up and engage, no matter how late they may feel they are in the process.

It's also important to check in with participants during your live launch as often as you can. The more touch points and the more direct interaction you have with prospects, the more results they'll get, and the easier your close will be with more revenue and money in the bank for you. You'll also be creating a stronger bond with greater reciprocity. Ultimately, it's a bigger ROI for you.

Make sure y... ...with your ...

emphasizing that the incentives are based ...

and being present. This builds the accountability level. Plus, it adds fun and excitement because everyone loves giveaways. Again, "homework" may or may not be how you couch the action steps you want participants to take to get results. Align it with your industry so that it makes sense. Regardless what you name it, it is an engagement tool for them to take action and get a new result. Always remember that at the heart of the Live Launch Method is using your own intuition and the freedom to be present with your group in the way that works for you.

Ensure that you're paying attention and cultivating conversations. Take and use what participants share to adjust and alter your own language and presentation or communication style. You always want to meet your audience where they are and give them what they need. This has an incredible impact on your conversions.

Use their language. Address their concerns. Meet them where they are.

Finally, after your live launch challenge, there are steps to take. The blitz model following the five-day challenge helps you scoop up about 50 percent more sales. This is a short, intense event that is like a catch-up plan for those leads and prospects who did not get through the first five-day event. It's a great opportunity for you to get another revenue boost and has a real ROI impact for the launch you've just completed.

You can connect with prospects in personal consultations, conduct overflow events, and continue to engage in the chat. These are ways that automatically set you up for your next cycle. When you're in the rhythm of the Live Launch Method, you're always in either pre-launch nurturing, in the launch itself, or in post-launch follow-up. All three provide opportunities for you to continue to sell, so you will get to the point at which there are sales closing and revenue coming into your business every single day.

Getting Live Launch Results

- Always remember that human connection is your super power.
- Live sessions should last 20-45 minutes, depending on the topic you're covering.
- Keep engagement going and growing, and check in with participants regularly.
- The more touch points you have, the more results they'll get, which ultimately means more money in the bank for you.
- Use a two-day blitz for those leads who did not complete the initial five-day launch.

Don't miss a single detail of your launch prep. Download our free Definitive Live Launch Planner Guide and get ready to make six-figure leaps in your business with each and every launch you execute!
www.kellyroachcoaching.com/livelaunchplanner

Chapter Seven

Steal These Strategies for Live Launch Success

Nothing gets me more excited than watching clients who have struggled for years finally embrace the power of the Live Launch Method and everything we teach inside the Unstoppable Entrepreneur program. Usually within just a couple of months (sometimes weeks) of joining the program, they skyrocket their results and return to tell their own stories. The full circle movement of that is incredibly gratifying and makes all those years of wanting to pull my hair out worth the struggle. While the focus of this book has been how to leverage the power of the Live Launch Method to grow your own business by six figures and beyond, I know you are probably thinking, "Yeah, but will it work for me?" So, I wanted to share some of the incredibly powerful stories of clients who have used the Live Launch Method to give you a deeper sense of what's possible.

Tara Antler joined the Tribe of Unstoppables Facebook group for one of our Live Launch Method workshops. During our launch, she decided to join us inside the Unstoppable Entrepreneur program so she could get the education, coaching, support, and accountability she needed to make multiple six-figure leaps in her business. After listening to countless Unstoppable Entrepreneur success stories, she told me from the start that she'd be one of my next success stories and here she is!

Tara has been an intuitive healer and soul coach for 17 years. As a coach in this capacity, she helps people connect to their higher self by clearing out the "ick and the stick," so they can gain clarity step into their purpose and create a life that is completely fulfilling.

Like me, Tara and her team tried many other things to scale their business. She had joined several other coaching programs. While she admits she learned something from all of them, when it came time to launch, the result was always the same... crickets. Tara explains, "We really put forth the best stuff, but then very little happened. It was so frustrating. The online world was new to us because we were used to doing the one-on-one sessions and running retreats for groups with in-person interactions." Like so many in the online world, Tara and her team were at their wits end with traditional launch methods.

As Tara's family grew, leveraging the online opportunity became more and more of a priority. She knew something had to change, including systemization, simplification, and "cutting the fluff." Going direct certainly seemed to be the key. "We'd developed a meditation trainer program because clients were asking for it, and it was coming at us full force. I was really scared to go online with it because we'd done it before and it didn't work. I didn't want to put in all the energy and effort, especially when we didn't have a lot of, if any, available time." Tara knew that maximizing their effort was critical but didn't know how to do it. She admits to having thrown up her hands.

"I put it up to the universe and said, 'You have to show me how to make this happen with ease and efficiency in a way that will honor us and our kids'." That's when she learned about the Live Launch Workshop through a Facebook ad. In reading the ad, she clearly identified with our own frustrations regarding failed launches, so she joined us. The universe had answered, and Tara stepped out in faith, keeping her end of the bargain.

Once inside, Tara knew she had stumbled on something that was going to be life (and business) changing. Tara continues, "I got so much out of the five days, and I was more productive in those five days than I'd been in the entire year prior. I had a long list, and in one day, I cleared off 22 items from the list… and patted myself on the back for it!" When the time came to join the Unstoppable Entrepreneur program, she knew it was for her but had some fear around making another investment.

The financial aspect of joining the Unstoppable Entrepreneur wasn't a huge hurdle as they'd done many other coaching programs at the $1,000 to $1,200 per month price point. Her big concern was, however, getting an actual return on her investment. Tara ultimately decided it was worth taking the leap and echoes what so many who have been through the FREE workshop have said, "I got more out of the free five days than I did in an entire year in a paid $1,400 per month program."

Despite her nagging concern about whether this would be a program just like all the others, she felt there was something different this time. So she took the leap and joined the Unstoppable Entrepreneur. Tara sensed that the financial investment would be recouped quickly… and it was. She immediately started taking action and began to gain some real momentum. The Unstoppable Entrepreneur helped her to cut through all the b/s that, in the past, had her stuck in the trivial details. The Live Launch Method and what she was learning inside the Unstoppable Entrepreneur program brought it all together in a way that was simple, straightforward, and streamlined.

Tara found an unmatched level of support with daily group calls inside the Unstoppable Entrepreneur program. Other programs did not offer her the same access. Nor did they have someone checking in as an accountability coach, which Tara found to be pivotal in her growth. "I could simply reach out and say, 'I'm stuck.' Knowing that I had availability to do that was a huge weight lifted off of me. I appreciated knowing that I wouldn't be left sitting by myself trying to figure it out without getting anything done."

Today, Tara and her team enjoy launching and closing clients every day in a way that serves her prospects, builds her brand, and allows her to scale with ease while doing dance parties during her launch. With two launches down, Tara's team closed $50,000 in their first launch and $72,000 in their second one. That's a six-figure stream of recurring income added to her bottom line with four to six launches left for the year! After years of launching with no real results, Tara now has a proven system to make her seven-figure dreams a reality.

The power of the Live Launch Method is now the fuel powering Tara's rocket ship. The training, coaching and accountability she receives inside of the Unstoppable Entrepreneur is like mission control for her rocket ship. Her trip around the moon and back has just started, and we can't wait to see where she goes next.

Like Tara, I have spent thousands on coaching and personal development. My team and I are consumers in our own market. We've paid for all the courses and tried all the methods. Nothing is as powerful as the Live Launch Method for entrepreneurs who want to make massive leaps in their business, year after year. Many of my clients have the same hesitation Tara did – having already invested $10,000, $20,000, $50,000 or more in coaching without seeing any real ROI, so there's a real reluctance to invest again. Your prospects will likely have a similar feeling about with you, and that's why it is so, so important to deliver more in your five-day launch for free than they've gotten out of paid programs in the past.

Another important point that Tara raised is the freedom the Live Launch Method provides because Tara has a dialed-in system to convert many new prospects at once and a recurring-revenue model set up, she can enjoy the freedom she started her business to enjoy.

For Tara, after just one month in the program, she was totally sold. on the Live Launch Method saying, "We're excited to repeat the process! People love the engagement, and it feels like a family."

Tara is just like you. She bet on herself, implemented the system with fidelity, and reaped the rewards. You too can do the same by leveraging what you've learned in this book. It will take work and courage and a commitment to see your ideal clients successful, but it's entirely possible!

Fastest ROI

Some of our clients take a few months to get the ball rolling, while others see a massive ROI immediately like our client Jessica Rhodes and her business partner, Margy Feldhun. Jessica and Margy are the co-owners of Interview Connections, a company that specializes in booking six-, seven-, and eight-figure entrepreneurs as guests on podcasts to grow their visibility, build their thought leadership and make more sales. In fact, their podcast booking agency is the first one ever created and is completely dominant in their industry. Despite an incredibly specific niche, and a done-for-you service as an offer, the Interview Connections ladies still saw incredible results using the Live Launch Method. However, Jessica was reluctant to use the Live Launch Method, so she dove into other areas of the Unstoppable Entrepreneur program first. Despite having significant sales experience, she leveraged a few of the trainings in our portal around closing high-ticket sales, specifically our One Conversation Close training.

As a result of using what she learned in the One Conversation Close, Jessica closed a sale and in a week recouped her investment in the program. She learned how to ask the right questions and use the responses in selling to her prospect. Here's what she had to say: "Now I ask, 'What is one concern or hesitation you have when looking to hire an agent to represent you for booking interviews?' The insight I got was amazing because my prospects were authentically sharing their concerns, and that allowed me to proactively put their mind at ease by explaining how our process would address their concern."

She also learned that she was diving in too soon to explain her service, including all of the packages and price points. It was far too confusing for people. The solution was to stop at that point in the call and ask, "Do you have any questions for me?" When they ask about pricing and procedures, Jessica now knows she'll likely close the deal. Not only did Jessica use the One Conversation Close to recoup her investment in UE in one week, she continued to book more clients during her first month in the program, significantly increasing her sales as a result. All this prior to launching.

Although reluctant, Jessica explains that they started a Facebook group that has literally helped her and Margy exponentially scale their sales using the Live Launch Method. They've had two launches, and closed six figures in both of those launches. Leveraging the Live Launch Method and what they learned in UE helped Jessica and Margy hit the seven-figure mark last year, and they haven't looked back since. Their new goal is to 10x their income, and the Live Launch Method is at the heart of their growth strategy.

First Live Launch Nets $300K

Michelle Bosch is the co-creator of the Land Profit Generator program, a program in which they teach participants how to purchase land for 25 cents on the dollar and then sell for 60, 80 or 100 percent of market value. It's similar to flipping houses, but they only deal with land to eliminate the complications that come with houses and structures. While land flipping might not seem like the most obvious niche for a successful launch, Michelle and her husband, Jack have absolutely blown it out of the water with two launches that brought in over $300,000 each!

"The Live Launch Method and the Unstoppable Entrepreneur program have given me and my team so much… in so little time." As soon as Michelle heard the Live Launch Method was done inside a Facebook group, her interest was piqued, since she'd already been nurturing a Facebook group. Michelle explains, "We were already very passionate about engaging on a daily basis and we'd already grown the group that way. Kelly shared that the Live Launch Method creates value for the members, and that's what we're really about. However, we already had our summer program planned and a live event on the books, so I had someone on my team join Kelly's Live Launch Workshop. She took incredible notes and assured me that it would be a perfect fit for our group."

Michelle's team member started creating the homework, but they still weren't certain what their offer would be. Their Facebook group had about 5,000 members. When they announced their live launch workshop was open for registration, she expected to have about 150 to 200 registrations. Two days into the promotion period, they had over 800 registrations. "I thought maybe we'd be in over our heads with a group of that size, so we got Kelly and her team's support, by joining the Unstoppable Entrepreneur program immediately. We didn't want to screw it up because I knew it could be a huge revenue-generating event. Her team rallied around us, and I never had such an incredible level of support. I paid $7,000 for the program on a Tuesday, and by the following Wednesday when our shopping cart closed, we made $300,000."

Michelle believes that any entrepreneur can get it done by watching and implementing the self-taught steps, but to make use of the team allows you to really maximize your efforts. After their first wildly successful launch, they did a second one with a pop-up group, spawned off of their original group, that included completely cold leads. "Everything that could have possibly gone wrong in that second launch went wrong. We were sick, had technology issues, and Facebook acted up a bit. But it was still a $50,000 launch to completely cold traffic. None of the participants really knew us before."

The Live Launch Method is now a key part of their business strategy. They've launched a third time and brought in another $300,000 in sales. "The ingredients of simplicity, intuition, and connecting with your audience are so important to us. The real estate industry is very 'noisy' with other programs and products. Using this methodology and strategy, we're really able to connect with the right prospects."

Michelle and her team really enjoy the Live Launch approach because it allows them to really get to know people and connect. In turn, that creates the goodwill they seek to establish and the value they want to deliver. "We're big believers in servant leadership, so this completely matched our mindset. We're able to do well while doing good for others."

The live launch gave inactive clients a reason to re-engage with Michelle and her team, and it re-energized them to buy again. "We had the perfect opportunity to bring value to these people again. It afforded me the opportunity to give the best of me to get the best of them. And we believe the key to prosperity is simplicity and that simplicity is a key component of the Live Launch Method."

A fun fact about Michelle's first launch: After the first couple of days during her launch, she sent over a voice memo asking for some advice on how to maximize sales during her open cart period. I helped her put together a bundle with some things her company already offered, and it made a $75,000 difference. ONE voice memo discussion through Facebook brought in $75,000! The Unstoppable Entrepreneur program has helped Michelle and her husband bring in close to $700,000 over a period of a few months. I would say that is well worth her $7,000 investment

Tara's story and her net gain of $30,000 in the first month is not an exception within the Unstoppable Entrepreneur program. Jessica and Margy's quick ROI is not a fluke. Michelle generating over $300,000 in revenue with the Live Launch Method, twice, while incredible will not be the last of its kind for our clients. The Live Launch Method is simply a tool that enables hard-working, laser-focused entrepreneurs to leverage human connection and make tons of money serving their prospects.

We hear repeatedly that using the Live Launch Method and joining the Unstoppable Entrepreneur program is the best decision our clients have ever made. Now you can use this incredibly powerful strategy to do the same for your business.

Download our free Definitive Live Launch Planner Guide to map out your own six-figure leaps at:

www.kellyroachcoaching.com/livelaunchplanner

Chapter Eight

7 Critical Questions ANSWERED to Help You Maximize Your Live Launch Results

I've covered a ton of information throughout this book about how you can use the Live Launch Method to grow your business by six and even seven figures. Because I want you to be able to really put this into use easily in your business, I'm including this Q&A chapter as a handy reference for you to double check information once you've completed reading.

I want you to generate incredible revenue in month one exactly the way Tara and others did.

What do we do with our group members between live launches?

In a word, "nurture." This is really the fun part and keeps your audience engaged. Use a weekly live show as an ongoing touch point. There will be no shortage of content for this. For example, someone in the real estate space may give tips on creating curb appeal, staging, listing and selling quicker, etc. If you're a business coach, you can present strategies on how your members can increase profitable results. If you're a relationship coach, you can address the simple changes your members can make to create the life they want. In the Unstoppable Entrepreneur program, we present a weekly "market domination checklist" for members to follow on an ongoing basis.

The weekly live show is the key to nurturing your people and keeping that human connection. It ensures that you have prospects who are warm and really ready to sign up for your program, product, or service every single day. In fact, closing sales every day is one of the core principles that we teach in the Unstoppable Entrepreneur program. Your launches will serve as your big bursts and leaps forward when you're onboarding dozens or more clients. The nurturing activities, like your weekly live show, continue to bring prospects to the consultation point and then conversion.

What if I provide a service that doesn't include a recurring program?

There are probably many entrepreneurs who think they fall into this category. Maybe you're a photographer, and right now, you're really busy but you don't have a stream of recurring income. You're working every day to get new customers. In the Unstoppable Entrepreneur program, we work with service-based business owners to actually develop a recurring-revenue package. You need to start every month with baseline revenue that exceeds the previous month, and we want to help you achieve that. It's a big no-no to wake up on the first of the month with no idea how you'll achieve at least as much as you did previously. Being in that constant cycle of finding customers and then serving customers, only to start again every month is the cause of incredible stress for any business owner. Moreover, you'll never grow your business and achieve the financial and time freedom that you want.

We help you develop a recurring-revenue offer in which a customer can sign up to work with you once but that generates the opportunity for you to get paid repeatedly with no real additional effort.

What if I'm a "solo-preneur" without a team to support me?

When I started my live launches, there were only two of us, so I know you can employ the Live Launch Method without a big team.

One of the cool things taking place now is that we have many Unstoppable Entrepreneur members who are virtual assistants (VA) who are learning the Live Launch Method. They are effectively "teams for hire" that you can bring on in an ad hoc or as needed basis, either during the week of your launch or also during the week before or after to help you with the burst of activity that is going to occur. Using contractors is a great way to hire help only when it's needed as you are just starting out, so you avoid a huge investment or long-term commitment. This way, you'll be getting people who've been trained in the Live Launch Method approaches and strategies. They'll know exactly what needs to be done and the support you need to convert sales.

So, yes: You can do this alone, but the goal, of course, is to use this methodology to grow your business in such a way that you will need to bring on other team members to continue to deliver and to continue to grow the business… as quickly as possible.

What if I'm not sure about my offer or flagship program?

So you've learned the Live Launch Method and can clearly see the benefit, but you're wondering about your offer or maybe you haven't even developed your flagship program yet. This is why the Unstoppable Entrepreneur program is so valuable. We get on a call with you and help you carve out the program that makes sense for you to offer, help price and name it, and coach you on the steps you need to take.

In fact, the sooner in your business venture you join the program, the better. We can help you avoid all of the typical start-up mistakes that many entrepreneurs make. Additionally, we can, from the very beginning, determine how you can create multiple streams of income, so you can grow your business and have the freedom to generate revenue without being completely tied to your business 24/7. It typically includes a high-ticket offer in which you're one-to-one with customers and a high-volume offer that will allow you to scale your business without taking a lot of your time.

How will the Live Launch Method work for my business?

The Live Launch Method can be put to use in any business or industry. We continue to have a really disparate group of people, and all are using it successfully. Some are in the personal or business coaching space, but it's not limited to coaching. As you read in the previous chapter, Jessica created her business around booking podcast guests – quite the specific niche, and she's doing really well growing her business. Those in health and wellness or fitness coaching are discovering that this method absolutely rocks. Ditto lawyers, doctors, pest control providers, financial advisors, salon owners, network marketers, photographers… anyone and everyone. Some clients are real estate agents or doing other sorts of land acquisition. No one of these businesses or industries overlap or really have much in common… other

> *Remember: Nothing changes until you do. Take the next step and make the commitment.*

than the fact that the Live Launch Method is allowing the entrepreneurs to skyrocket their growth and bank accounts.

No matter what space you serve, in the Unstoppable Entrepreneur program, we can help you create the programs that make sense for your particular business and uncover the strategies that will enable you to have incredible success and growth. I assure you, this is not a pipe dream. It simply needs your commitment to learn the skills you need to grow your business by six or seven figures and pop the bubble that may currently surround you, limiting your thinking and imagination. Get out of the box and do something different… the thing that will put you in a category of one, so you blow away your competition!

Additionally, the interaction within the group between entrepreneurs in various industries is really wonderful. There are some commonalities, and we often see brainstorming between members who share what they've done in their space only to see that strategy tweaked as needed to be really successful in another completely unrelated industry. There's brainstorming to help you cut through the noise that invades every industry. There can be a lot of competition because anyone can launch a business – there's no barrier to entry, but not everyone, in fact very few, will be successful. The Live Launch Method is the perfect way to set yourself apart from all the "me too" marketers that are all too common in every industry.

What should my price point be?

First things first. Many entrepreneurs do not price their programs and services high enough when they're starting out. Their thinking is that they have to offer low-ball pricing to get customers in the first place. I'll strongly caution you against this approach. Why? With low pricing, you'll be attracting the types of customers you don't want. That makes it much, much harder to sell. And then when you do close, you'll end up filling your calendar with clients you do not have an interest in serving. They're buying on price. You want them to buy your expertise. Ideally, your flagship program should be priced between $350 and $850 or more monthly. The lower your price, the lower the quality of leads you'll attract.

You'll be demonstrating your expertise during your live launch, so prospects already know what they're getting. Plus, you'll be providing what they need to get results immediately, and they'll get more from your free workshop than with other programs they've already paid for. Charge accordingly! If you're still unsure what you should charge, setting price points and helping you create packages that are worthy of high price points is what we cover in the Unstoppable Entrepreneur program (www.uerevolution.com) as well as marketing and targeting the right prospects – those who will pay what you charge.

What about a three-month program vs. ongoing coaching?

We'll help you determine if this approach is really right for your particular business and then help you set up your live launches to support this approach. However, experience indicates that you are far better able to help your clients and customers get the results they want and need with a six- or twelve-month program. Keep in mind the foundation of serving and helping your clients succeed. When your clients succeed, your business grows. Chances are you see the vast majority of the people in your space launching short-term programs that get clients very minimal results. If you want to become peerless in your industry, step up to the plate and work with your clients over the long-term to provide a substantial and lasting result.

Download our free Definitive Live Launch Planner Guide to map out your own six-figure leaps at: www.kellyroachcoaching.com/livelaunchplanner

Chapter Nine

5 Open Cart Essentials to Nail the Sale and Scale, Scale, Scale

Congratulations! You are the 1% of the 1% who are actually following through until completion and ready to ROCK your live launch! In this chapter, I am going to walk you through five of the most important open cart rituals, strategies and mindsets to help you nail the sale and scale, scale, scale your business online.

1. The Value Stack

I am not the originator of this concept by any stretch of the means. The value stack is an essential piece of presenting your offer and has been for quite some time. What I will tell you about the live launch presentation of the stack is that it is critical that your audience hear it five or *more* times.

I emphasize this because I see so many failed launches using other methods that could have worked… BUT the prospects simply did not get the information they needed enough times, clearly enough to make an educated decision, so they did nothing at all. One of the big reasons why the Live Launch Method works so well is that your audience gets to spend real time with you over a period of days not a single hour or on a few recorded videos.

You want to make sure you spell out every element of the program, what it teaches, the transformation it creates, and the outcome prospects will experience over and over again.

When you go into your five days of selling, you are continuing to teach and add value, but in every session, you are spelling out specifically the full value stack describing the program in detail.

2. Have Your Clients Tell THEIR STORIES

Oner of the biggest drivers of sales during your launch will be your clients. It's wonderful for your prospects to hear from you why your program is the best of the best, but what they really want is to hear from regular people like themselves that YES this will work for you.

We recommend a combination of live interviews of clients and solo presentations during which the clients reveal their stories, their successes, and the results they have achieved with your program.

3. Scarcity and Urgency

You are 100 percent in control of the scarcity and urgency involved in each round of your launch. That being said, people by nature self-sabotage by procrastinating. You have to give prospects a good reason to *take action now*.

You can do this by raising the price after the initial offer, removing certain bonuses on a set date, opening only a limited number of spots, etc.

You have to remember that no matter how good your program or sales pitch is people are people and you have to motivate urgent action now by creating parameters that drive this.

Make sure you plan out all of these elements prior to your launch.

4. Consultations Matter

Depending on your price point and the power of your pitch, you may need to bring people into consultations vs. driving them to a sales page.

Don't wait for them to come to you. When you are in open cart, make sure in every video, you mention that either you or your team are available for consults.

Many times when someone is about to make a large investment, they have nerves or just one or two small lingering questions. Having a quick five- to ten-minute conversation with a lead can be the tipping point for many, many extra sales in each launch.

Consult don't coach. During the consultations, ensure that you keep the conversation strategic not tactical regarding their situation, but emotional connection is the true goal.

You want to help people, above all else, feel calm and certain that they can make this investment confidently and that your program is their solution.

5. Lean in

The biggest risk in a launch is that, if and when you don't see the immediate response, you want to pull back. Do not, I repeat, do not pull back. The vast majority of your sales will be in the last 48 hours, **but** this will not happen if you don't follow through.

Many entrepreneurs begin to panic when they transition to the sale and engagement drops and viewers drop and things quiet down. This is totally normal. People are thinking, praying, discerning, speaking with their spouses and so much more.

You cannot react and change the schedule or plan to do less because things get quiet. In fact, this is when you should think about doing more. You have to allow people to go through all of the psychological steps necessary to wrap their head around making a $10,000 or $20,0000 investment in their business.

Finally, remember that the level of certainty that you convey will be the mirror you will receive from your audience. They are by default scared, uncertain, overwhelmed and maybe even confused. You have to lead them, strongly encourage them and give them the full support required to make an educated decision that will have a profound impact on their life.

Download our free Definitive Live Launch Planner Guide to map out your own six-figure leaps at: www.kellyroachcoaching.com/livelaunchplanner

Chapter Ten

Case Studies

In the following pages, I'm sharing case studies from clients who have used the Live Launch Method with varying degrees of incredible success. In each, you'll find they've explained their ideal client, offer, and Facebook group along with their comments about the process. Plus, I've included their sites and contact information as well.

While the Live Launch Method can be used to build *any* type of business at *any* stage, there is one common thread that runs through all of these case studies: these clients put in the work.

If you are willing to do the work, follow the methodology, and show up for your people, six-figure results are absolutely within reach and will likely become your new norm.

J. Massey – Cashflow Diary

Real Estate Investor, Educator

$500k in fewer than 90 days!

Ideal Client: Men and women who want to start investing in real estate, build a portfolio, create a six-plus-figure stream of income somewhat passively, and think short-term rentals might be their best route.

The Offer: Year-long, short-term rental business incubator with three phases of content to walk new investors step-by-step through the process of starting their short-term rental business and scaling their short-term rental business. The program includes an extensive membership portal with training for every level of investor, monthly accountability calls, weekly group coaching calls, a dedicated app, and the support of leading experts in the short-term rental and real estate world.

Facebook Group: J. had a large group of prospects to start with. His group had over 10k members, so he didn't have to spend any time building his group. He had been nurturing the group weekly with Q+A sessions during which members could call in and get their questions answered by J. himself.

J. was already running a seven-figure business when he stumbled on the Live Launch Method, but he wanted a simpler way to launch that would leverage his strengths (live video) and help him connect with his people. He was launching over and over and over, had no recurring revenue set up, and was always starting over again. The Live Launch Method, The Unstoppable Entrepreneur, and Legacy Leaders have helped J. create recurring revenue (over $50k/month) and consistently launch to multiple six figures while serving his clients at a far higher level than he ever dreamed possible.

Comments: "Working with Kelly, using the Live Launch Method is family-tree changing. I've never been able to serve my clients at such a high level while growing my income so exponentially! I did not think that another person could have the level of impact, could move the needle in my business, the way that this has moved the needle."

Website: cashflowdiary.com
Instagram: @cashflowdiary
Facebook Group: Short Term Rental Mastery || Cashflow Diary

Michelle Bosch

Land Flipping, Land Profit Generator

Three $300K+ launches with unparalleled connection

Ideal Client: Beginning real estate investors or experienced house investor who is tired of the competition in the housing world.

The Offer: Michelle's offer was composed of a course, yearly software subscription, and a two-day, hands-on workshop that walked students through their land flipping methodology and software. The price point was $6,500.

Facebook Group: Michelle and her husband, Jack had already built her Facebook group to over 5,000 people and utilized this foundation plus DMs to further engage her community. Michelle had a team in place to help with her launch.

The Live Launch Method helped Michelle and Jack produce over $300k in sales in their first launch. It also impacted thousands of people inside their group and was a process they enjoyed using!

Comments: "The connection we were able to establish with our students and the goodwill inside of the group was unparalleled. We saw so many who didn't take our offer or just bought the course but were able to get started with their first deal making between $5k-$25k and see their lives become unstuck and transformed because that first deal sculpted their spirit and will eventually enable them to afford our higher level coaching."

Website: landprofitgenerator.com/webclass
Instagram: @michellboschofficial
Facebook Group: Land Profit Lab

Kelly Ruta – Kelly Ruta International

Psychotherapist, Speaker, Coach

From $250k/year to $330K in one quarter!

Ideal Client: Female, service-based entrepreneur, spiritual, open-minded, highly self-aware, extremely ambitious but bumps up against money/visibility/team/confidence ceilings in an effort to scale. She often either hustles to burnout or procrastinates as a result of self-doubt and perfectionism. She has deep desires for "so much more" and has invested in programs to grow her business but is realizing she is the bottleneck and working with me will help her create the mindset mastery and personal command that will allow her to get results out of everything else she's investing in.

The Offer: Group coaching program – Becoming Limitless Entrepreneurial Mindset Mastery Program. The program is currently nine months and $8,500 but will be moving to 12 months and $10,000.

Facebook Group: When Kelly joined the Unstoppable Entrepreneur program and decided to do her first launch, she had ***zero*** people in her Facebook group. She grew her group to 300 people in three weeks using Facebook ads. Her ad spend during her first launch was $5,000 and during her second launch was $4,600.

Kelly had used challenges prior to learning the Live Launch Method with varying degrees of success. While she was able to make sales, she was not able to leverage her on-camera skills the way she knew she could.

Comments: "The Live Launch Method *finally* allowed me a way to showcase and position my expertise in a niche where there is a serious gap in expertise and to get paid in alignment with my 25 years of education, training, practice and experience. I went from not being able to break $200K to making over $300K in four months."

Website: https://kellyruta.com/
Instagram: @kellysruta
Facebook Group: Limitless Entrepreneurs

Kate & Chris Kenney – Chris Kenney Coaching

Business Consulting

Quarter of a million in sales!

Ideal Client: Ambitious coaches, consultants, and entrepreneurs who want to rapidly accelerate their income and increase their impact in the world by learning to position, package, and sell high-ticket programs.

The Offer: "High-Ticket Sales Mastery Mentorship" a 12-month group coaching program. The cost of the offer was $1,250/month or $13,500 paid in full.

Facebook Group: Kate and Chris launched to a group of 301. They built the group slowly and started organically. Eventually, they accelerated the growth and brought in an ads team, who ran ads in the three weeks running up to their launch (doubling the group size from 150 to 301). Their total ad spend and maintenance was $20k, and they did have a team in place to help them prior to and during their launch.

Chris had done most of his selling prior to the Live Launch Method from stage and webinars. However, the idea of no funnels, webinars or tech – and being able to pivot and teach in response to the audience – was highly attractive to the Kenney's. In their first launch, they closed $240k in sales.

Comments: "We made a quarter of a million dollars in sales with our first live launch – with only 300 people in our group! In the month prior to the launch, Chris and I were also literally away from the business for three weeks – both speaking on stages in South Africa (one week), followed by a week completely 'unplugged' on a trip-of-a-lifetime safari, followed by running a retreat in London, UK. We were back literally just two weeks before the launch."

Website: chriskenneycoaching.com
Instagram: @thechriskenney
Facebook Group: Sales Mastery Inner Circle

Kendall Summerhawk – Kendall Summerhawk

Business Coaching

$150k using the Live Launch Method

Ideal Client: Women who want to start coaching female entrepreneurs but don't already have a complete step-by-step set of their own content system ready to go or the time to create one.

The Offer: Certified Coach Training as a Money Breakthrough Business Coach. It is a $6,000 investment, including done-for-you coaching content and branding as your own worksheets, coaching exercises, plus certified coach training. Tuition includes forever access to the certified coach training plus a one-year membership in the coaching business incubator.

Facebook Group: Kendall saw the Live Launch Method as an opportunity to exponentially grow her reach and the number of women enrolling in her certification program. She started her Facebook group for her live launch and grew it organically to 300 members in two weeks! She hired a small, part-time team to help prior to and during her launch.

The Live Launch Method has given Kendall a clear plan with 'payday dates' on the calendar for an entire year. It's focused her marketing efforts on growing her Facebook group, exponentially increasing her sales and her impact. Her team has enrolled as many people in just 75 days as they did in a total of eight months last year.

Comments: "My first wow moment was seeing people enrolling into certification training within 24 hours of open cart. I was confident going into the launch that we would do well but to see it happening felt amazing. My second wow moment was seeing the incredible quality of clients coming into certification training. They are my perfect clients!"

Website: kendallsummerhawk.com
Twitter: kendallcoach
Facebook Group: Tribe of Courageous Coaches

GeNienne Samuels – Sideline Prep

Coaching for Professional Cheerleaders

$100k launch with only $350 spent on Facebook ads

Ideal Client: Female cheerleaders between the ages of 17-32. They love to dance and perform and would like to make a professional cheerleading team.

The Offer: A four-month group coaching program that includes ten virtual trainings, live accountability calls twice a month, accountability check-ins with a coach two times per month, unlimited Q&A in private Facebook group, challenges, an accountability partner, dance instruction videos, a makeover session with a coach, two one-on-one sessions with a coach, unlimited feedback on videos and photos. The cost for the four-month program is $1,997.

Facebook Group: GeNienne had *zero* people in her Facebook group when she joined The Unstoppable Entrepreneur. When she started her challenge, she had 288 people in the group which grew to 375 by the end of her challenge week. It took her about a month and a half to build to that level.

Prior to using the Live Launch Method, GeNienne had used webinars and traditional launch methods for her program but wasn't getting the massive results she would have liked to. However, after using the Live Launch Method, she had her biggest launch to date with 32 new sign-ups in addition to the 22 ladies who had joined just prior to the launch. With 54 women in the program, GeNienne brought in over $100k with only $350 in ad spend and the help of one VA.

GeNienne was blown away by her results and by how much she actually enjoyed the process!

Comments: "Launching doesn't have to be hard or stressful. With the Live Launch Method it can be fun, energizing, and exciting. You can create a journey for your customers to take… one that educates and entertains them along the way. You're able to 'show off' your success stories in a non-boastful way, utilizing these stories to teach lessons but also gain and increase credibility. You're also able to learn more about your audience… their needs, wants, and desires so you can better serve them.

"I had my biggest launch ever for my Pro Cheer Playbook Program. I was able to connect with more people in a deeper way, leading to more sign-ups for my coaching program than ever before. I now have more money coming in every month to help with expenses, bills, and living!"

Website: sidelineprep.com
Instagram: @sidelineprep
Facebook Group: Prep to Pro - Cheer and Dance

Jessica Rhodes & Margy Feldhun – Interview Connections

Podcast Booking Agency (Done-for-You Service)
$125k in Sales of a done-for-you service

Ideal Client: Service-based, online entrepreneurs generating at least $300k in annual revenue. They have built their business through referrals and word of mouth and are ready to get more exposure in front of their ideal clients.

The Offer: Our Center of Influence Program offers 48 podcast bookings over a period of 12 months. This service also includes a month-long discovery process with their booking agent team and two consult calls. There are two bonuses for those who signed up during the launch: $1,000 discount and quarterly group coaching calls for signing up during the live launch. The cost of their package was $1,367/month or $15,400 paid in full.

Facebook Group: Jess and Margy started their Facebook group for the purpose of using the Live Launch Method. They built it organically at first for two to three months in order to exceed the 300 mark for their launch. In their first launch, the brought in over $100k with no ads. They started ads for their second launch and built their group significantly. Without the help of a VA or social seller, Jess and Margy did 28 consults, closed nine clients who exceeded $15k+ for $135, in sales. Their ad spend on the second launch was $3,656 plus the agency fee to run ads.

Where most would think this process couldn't work for a done-for-you service, Jess and Margy saw an opportunity. They realized they couldn't scale without a dialed-in way to nurture new leads in a one-to-many format. They couldn't rely solely on consults if they wanted to hit their revenue goals. So they curated a group of qualified leads and educated and served. They quickly realized their quickest path to growth was going to be leveraging the Live Launch Method and committed to launching six to eight times in 2020. With two $100k launches under their belt, they've brought on social sellers and are ready to exponentially increase their results.

Comments: "It has made it so much more fun to sell because most leads are now being nurtured by our content before getting on a sales call! We are also able to scale and grow so much faster. I love that we now have a place for prospects to go when they aren't ready for a sales call." ~ Jessica Rhodes

Website: interviewconnections.com
Instagram: @interviewconnections
Facebook Group: Guest Expert Profit Lab

Melissa Ricker

Online Biz Coach
Back-to-back multiple six-figure launches

Ideal Client: Online entrepreneurs (service providers, coaches, consultants, and course creators) looking to grow their brand and build out a value ladder, so they aren't stuck trading hours for dollars in 1:1 services.

The Offer: Melissa's offer consisted of the Funnel Boss Academy, $7,000 paid in full or $700/month for 12 months.

Facebook Group: Melissa started with 1,200 in a pop-up group for her live launch. Within three days, she was able to add 300 members to her Facebook group. She employed an OBM/social seller, three different Vas, and used Facebook ads, spending about $6,000 to reach her ideal audience size.

As a result of the Live Launch Method, Melissa went from $10-15k/month to now having back-to-back six-figure launches in three months. A total of 28 people joined her program, ten signed up live, and 15 the first day for the fast action bonus.

Comments: "I love the flexibility and how you're able to have your launch evolve as you evolve. I also love the team aspect of it and how that is actually a selling point."

Website: engineeredmotherhood.com
Instagram: melissaricker_funnelboss
Facebook Group: Irresistible Offer Bootcamp

Ryann Dowdy – Uncensored Consulting

Sales Coach
From non-existent to consistent five-figure months

Ideal Client: Ryann teaches sales to new, B2B service providers.

The Offer: A 12-month group coaching program that includes her sales training vault, 1:1 accountability, a private coaching community, and weekly group coaching calls. Ryann's current offer price is $300/month or $3,000 paid in full. This price is triple what it was when she joined The Unstoppable Entrepreneur.

Facebook Group: Ryann's first launch in January of 2019 had 250 people in it. It currently has 300+ people. Ryann has grown her group organically up until this point, using the strategies in the Unstoppable Entrepreneur. She ran her first launches with no help but brought on a VA and has just hired a social seller.

Ryann's growth has been incredible. In July of 2019, she reworked her offer and dialed in her Live Launch Method. Three weeks after giving birth, she launched her new program and had 20 prospects buy for a total of $48k in sales. She ended 2019 with over $100k in cash received with *over* $100k on the books for 2020 (before December 31st rolled around). In January of 2020, she launched again with a higher price point. She added another $29k to the books for 2020 using a pop-up group and is set to launch several more times in 2020. Ryann went from earning $1000/month in her business to making *over* six figures and growing! She is a true testament to the power of using the Live Launch Method and really committing to it as a launch strategy, over and over again.

Comments: "The Live Launch Method has helped me continue to launch my program in a fun way. It's literally transformed my business!"

Website: uncensoredconsulting.com
Instagram: @ryanndowdyuncensored
Facebook Group: Sales Skills for Women in Business

Kayla Paradis – Keeper of Keys

Yoga + Spirituality
Doubled her sales in one month!

Ideal Client: Women looking to live a more spiritually fulfilled and intuitively connected life.

The Offer: A group intuitive coaching program designed to connect women to spiritual and emotional healing. This three-month group coaching program was delivered live. The cost of the program was $1,100 for three months.

Facebook Group: At the time of her launch, Kayla had 125 people in her Facebook group. While that is smaller than we recommend, she did have a high level of engagement and an audience that fully bought in. She is currently growing her Facebook group organically for her next launch.

Despite starting with a small audience and a short offer, Kayla took imperfect action to make things happen. The call to action at the end of her launch was to book a consult call. Out of 125 people in her group, Kayla booked seven consult calls and closed five sales. For her, this was a huge increase in sales and she was over-the-moon excited. Kayla then used our Livenar model to book several more clients in the month following. She recently hired an assistant to help with her upcoming launches.

Comments: "I have doubled my sales within one month of joining. I continue to grow and learn along the way. I really feel this has created a fast track for success in my business!"

Website: Keeperofkeys.net
Instagram: @rparadispractice
Facebook Group: Keeper of Keys Collaborative

Baeth Davis – Hand Analyst, Inc.

Online Business Mentoring
$100k Launch after battling cancer

Ideal Client: Women 55+ who feel underutilized and want a business that allows them to live out their life purpose.

The Offer: Online group coaching with hand analysis, monthly group coaching calls, monthly accountability calls, and monthly webinars. Her program cost was $1,000/month, for a 12-month program.

Facebook Group: Baeth had 245 people in her Facebook group and added another 300 organically in one week using the methods we teach in The Unstoppable Entrepreneur. She had two coaches focused on nurturing new members, and a VA helping with admissions to the group.

In Baeth's first launch, she signed on 14 new clients for $14,000/month in recurring revenue and $168,000/year in sales. She then used our Livenar model to sign on seven more people for a total of $21,000/month and $252,000/year in sales.

Baeth was on the verge of quitting her business. She was struggling to make things work, tired of using traditional launch strategies that didn't work, and ready to experience a true breakthrough in her business. She had an incredible offer, lots of testimonials, and a team that was ready to make things happen. The Live Launch Method gave her the vehicle to exponentially grow her business and get back in the game.

Comments: Baeth obviously loved her results and was excited to realize that "social media is profitable and fun!"

Website: : yourpurpose.com
Instagram: Baethdavis
Facebook Group: Align to Your Design

Sara Longoria – Sara Longoria

Manifestation and Money Coaching
Creating consistent five-figure months

Ideal Client: Six- and seven-+-figure high-achieving entrepreneurs who want business and life to be easier, more in flow, and create more time and ease while learning to accomplish more and make more money.

The Offer: Year-long coaching program showing clients how to create what they want in life. Live group coaching calls and training modules.

Facebook Group: When she started her pre-launch, Sara had 120 people in her group. She did grow her group to 300 organically. Sara ran zero ads for her first launch, closed eight clients for a total of $40,000 in monthly recurring revenue. She had three part-time people helping her DM and sell during the launch!

Sara create five-figures in *recurring* revenue and enjoyed the process.

Comments: "The online world can be really up and down for many. Always looking for the next thing and wondering if next month is going to be as good as last month. I really wanted to retire my husband, and although I was making money, in his eyes it wasn't something we could count on every month... which left me at a place of trying to figure out how I could create $25k a month and know, without a doubt, it would stay consistent. Enter the Live Launch Method and Kelly Roach. This strategy allowed me to not only create consistent months like this but bring more ease to my business and get my product out to the world on a much bigger scale."

Website: saralongoria.com

Instagram: @saralongoria_
Facebook Group: Manifesting for Entrepreneurs

Diahana Barnes – Diahana Barnes Coaching

Business Success Strategist for Visionary Leaders
$25k in sales while creating a group coaching program that gave her more freedom

Ideal Client: Women looking to leave the corporate world or who have and heart-centered coaches, healers, entrepreneurs who are ready to build six-figure-plus businesses by being a harmonious CEO who builds with ease and grace.

The Offer: Six-month group coaching program for $2,500.

Facebook Group: It took Diahana about two weeks to get her Facebook group to the 300 mark. She did use ads, and spent $1,000 on them.

Diana had built her business to over six figures exclusively with 1:1 VIP clients. She was looking to scale and tried a bunch of different things with little success. Until she ran her first live launch, she hadn't successfully filled a group program. She was looking for scalability and wanted to create a powerful group program that didn't rely solely on her.

Comments: "It has changed my business significantly. I filled my first group program using the combination of speaking in person and the Live Launch Method with our first launch earning $5k.

"We tripled our revenue from December 2019 to January 2020 using the Live Launch Method and our last launch hit over $25k. This is huge for me… up until this point, I've grown the business fairly slowly, struggling to get past the low six-figure mark practically by myself through VIP clients."

Website: diahanabarnes.com
Instagram: @coachdiahana

Kimberly Olson – The Goal Digger Girl

Network Marketing + Business Coaching
Quarter-of-a-million-dollar launch + $30k recurring revenue

Ideal Client: Female entrepreneurs who are also moms and want to get to six figures in their network marketing business or create systems for duplication if they've already reached the six-figure mark.

The Offer: 6 Figure Breakthrough Business Academy – a six-month group coaching program designed to teach clients the simple systems and online strategies to sell, market, and duplicate on social media. Cost: $497/month or $2,485 paid in full.

Facebook Group: Kimberly had a Facebook group with about 4,000 people in it. She used paid ads and organic social media marketing to add an additional 1,000 people to her Facebook group for the ten days leading up to her live launch. She had one full-time person, my Operations Director, and two prior coaching clients help with her launch, including Facebook group engagement and DMing to close clients.

Prior to learning the Live Launch Method, Kimberly was doing random workshops (stand-alone webinars), 30-day bootcamps, eight-week bootcamps, private team 90-day programs, and private coaching. She was putting out a ***ton*** of content but was exhausted. What she was doing was not scalable at all. After using the Live Launch Method, she created $30k/month in ***recurring*** revenue, which was critical for her, since prior to joining The Unstoppable Entrepreneur, she was chasing new clients every single month.

Comments: "I stumbled upon Kelly Roach in November of 2019 and couldn't believe what she was teaching. I learned more in her Live Launch Method than I did in four years of business school. I knew by doing her program, I would learn true sales and marketing, along with ways to scale my business and not get burned out. When Kelly said to offer so much value in your launch that it would make those participating wonder what it would be like to work with me in my paid program, that was everything for me. I worked really hard on the content in the workbook that went with my launch and taught my heart out. This caused me to raise the bar for myself. I went all in and because of that, so are my students. It's really amazing."

Website: https://thegoaldiggergirl.com/
Instagram: @thegoaldiggergirl

Koni Scavella – Iconic Consulting

Business Strategist
$51K in recurring revenue with a group of 75

Ideal Client: Seasoned service-based entrepreneurs, CEOs and thought leaders (speakers, authors, coaches, consultants) earning six figures or more, with a team of fewer than ten people who want to scale to seven-plus-figures

The Offer: 12-month group coaching program, the Iconic Leadership Academy, VIP Strategy Session, Iconic Members Vault, SOAR membership, and 21-Day Mind Mastery program.

Facebook Group: When she decided to do a live launch, Koni had no group at all. She worked on growing her group, and in a few days, had 75 people in her group – 15 of whom were family and friends! She did not use ads on her first launch and didn't have any help.

Koni took messy action and launched with just her tiny group and completely on her own. In the month of December, when most businesses that work with other businesses are slowing down, Koni made $51k in sales.

She had worked with other coaches before and tried other methods but had little success. Despite her significant corporate background and years of experience, she struggled to sell one-to-many. The Live Launch Method gave her the methodology and confidence to bring her expertise to market and make massive leaps in her business.

Website: http://koniscavella.com/
Instagram: @koniscavella
Facebook Group: The Iconic Entrepreneur

Tara Antler – Ascension Academy of Light

Healing, Spirituality, Meditation
Over $150K of recurring revenue in two launches

Ideal Client: Primarily women between the ages 25 - 55 who are interested in meditation, yoga, crystals, self-help, intuition, and consciousness. These women want to live life on their own terms, and free themselves from the regular Monday - Friday, 9-5 grind. They want more abundance and to tap into and embody not only the Law of Attraction (so they can live in alignment with their Spiritual Self), they also want to continue to explore spirituality and new age topics.

Our ideal customers are similar to Gabby Bernstein's or Collette Baron Reid's clients.

The Offer: The first launch was for the Ascension Meditation Certification. This four-month certification cost $2,000 if paid in full or $2,300 in a payment plan. The second launch was for Tara's flagship offer, Thrive 365, a 12-month spiritual growth incubator that includes weekly training sessions, Q+A sessions daily, and monthly creation circles. The total pay in full cost is $5,723 or $530/month for 12 months.

Facebook Group: Tara had no Facebook group when joining us inside The Unstoppable Entrepreneur. She grew her group to 320 people in one week, organically. She had help from one person as she was growing her group.

Tara had tried launching in a variety of ways prior to using The Live Launch Method. She was overwhelmed and confused, always focusing on things that didn't seem to move the needle forward, including list building through online summits; funnels; five-day challenges; being an expert on other summits; and complicated and multi-step, evergreen automated webinar funnels. After having her twins, she couldn't afford to spend her time figuring out these complicated systems that yielded mediocre results. She was frustrated and overwhelmed feeling as though she couldn't crack the online marketing code, even though she had grown and run successful offline businesses.

Comments: "Oh my gosh! The Live Launch Method has been a dream! An answered prayer! *The* solution to everything we've ever dreamed of or knew was possible! We have launched two large programs in four months which resulted in over $58K in new income in one launch! And then our second launch happened just before Christmas, while we were moving to Mexico, packing our entire house, putting everything in storage. We launched our year incubator and made $96K between the five-day launch and our one-day blitz!

"We are excited when we launch now… instead of dreading what's to come. No more fear of putting in so much time, energy, and work and feeling disappointed with very low response or registration.

"Our kids are happy because we're not stressing about time, energy or *all* the tasks that used to be a requirement. They know that every six to eight weeks it's go-time for five days and then mommy and daddy can chill and relax and be with them 100 percent.

"It really has been *the best* business decision I've made in a loooooong time! And I've worked with a lot of other coaches and programs! This one is the icing on the cake, the cake and the party that goes along with it!"

Website: www.taraantler.com/
Instagram: @taraantler
Facebook Group: 5 Day Healing Challenge with Tara Antler

Danielle Cevallos – Firebrand Communication Strategies

Communication Strategist and Copywriter
Live launching a done-for-you service

Ideal Client: While Danielle currently works with seven- to eight-figure business owners who want to build a disruptive, iconic brand, at the time of her launch, she was working with service-based business owners.

The Offer: Danielle sold a monthly content package that included authority blogs, highly converting emails, and engagement-focused social media posts. The cost was $1,050/month.

Facebook Group: Danielle had a group of about 500 people when she first launched. She ran ads to her lead magnet then redirected people to her group for her launch. Her total ad spend was under $500, and she did very little to promote the workshop. She had the help of a part-time VA for community management.

Danielle was reluctant to launch because she provided a done-for-you service and wasn't sure of her ability to onboard and provide service to large quantities of people at once. Through the Unstoppable Entrepreneur and Legacy Leaders, she was able to get a team in place, so she could provide service to those who booked during her launch. She brought in $15k in recurring revenue, and the majority of those clients have extended their original contracts making the lifetime value generated by that launch over $50k.

Comments: "The Live Launch Method can truly work for anyone, with any type of goal. It's a simple way to serve potential clients and build a relationship based on trust. It is so simple and so powerful, that if you can just halfway implement – you will see results!"

Website: firebrandcommunicationstrategies.com
Instagram: @firebrandcom
Facebook Group: Firebrand Communication Strategies

Dr. Ranelli Williams – ERJ Services, LLC

Accounting
I was winging it and NOW I have structure!

Ideal Client: Service-based entrepreneurs scaling to multiple six figures.

The Offer: Ranelli's offer was the Elite Profit Masters Program, which includes bookkeeping, accountability, financial statement analysis, and profit strategy to ensure her clients get the desired result: more profits. The price point is $550 per month.

Facebook Group: Ranelli had about 400 people in her Facebook group. She grew her group organically and it took her about another month to add 200 additional people. She is now at 1,300 members after several months. Her team consisted of someone responsible for engagement during the launch and a VA to help with the small details of her launch.

Before the Live Launch Method, Ranelli was basically depending on referrals. She believed that the Live Launch Method was a way to provide focused value and show how her offer could get results. The Live Launch Method has helped Ranelli to strategically think about her ideal audience and restructure the focus of her group.

Comments: "My wow moment was the lesson of how much I did not have a structure in my business for continually bringing in clients. I was winging it, and now I have a structure."

Website: www.erjservices.com
Instagram: @drranelliwilliams
Facebook Group: Profitable Entrepreneurs Network

Evelyn Knight – Child Care Business Professionals

Child Care/Daycare
$30k in 2 weeks!

Ideal Client: Evelynn's ideal clients are existing daycare owners.

The Offer: She offered a membership with group coaching at $199 a month and one-on-one coaching at $1,500 a month.

Facebook Group: Evelyn's existing Facebook group consisted of 550 members, and she was able to add 300 members in a couple of weeks through DMs and messaging without the assistance of a team. A total of six daycare owners joined her program during her live launch with direct links and consult calls offered by Evelyn.

Comments: "As a start-up business, the Live Launch Method has helped me begin building from the ground up! Over the course of the Kelly's Live Launch Method, I could really see the difference in quality from the other methods I watched and learned. I was looking for something to use, but even $200 a month seemed like too much to me for other programs. Kelly's business structure, organization, and method were obviously superior to the other methods I was looking at even compared to some of the biggest names in the industry at the time!"

Website: www.childcarebusinessprofessionals.com
Instagram: @childcarebusinesscoach
Facebook Group: The ChildCare Business Coach

Stephanie Clairmont – The Leveraged Dietician

Dietician, Coach
From $100k years to $100k quarters

Ideal Client: Entrepreneurial health professionals who want to reduce 1:1 client appointments by offering a results-driven online group program in their practice, avoid burnout, and increase revenue.

The Offer: 12-month coaching program with training, templates, teaching, coaching, accountability, and all the tools needed to successfully offer, market and sell an online health or professional development program. The cost of the program was $625/month or $6,750 paid in full.

Facebook Group: Stephanie didn't have a Facebook group when she decided on her live launch, but grew her group to over 300 people using Facebook ads and organic methods in about six weeks. Her total ad spend was $,5000 for her launch. She had a VA help her through her launch.

Stephanie had been selling her offers using social media and webinars. She kept maxing out at around the $100k mark each year and couldn't break through that plateau. The Live Launch Method helped her not only break through that but serve her clients in a new, more effective way. Stephanie recently reported that using the Live Launch Method and the others we teach inside of the Unstoppable Entrepreneur, she closed more in the first quarter of 2020 than she did in all of 2019.

Comments: "Once the most recent live launch was complete, and I could debrief on the relationships that were made, the value that was provided to all, and the revenue that was produced, that was the ***wow*** moment for me. The capacity at which I can support all these new clients is exciting and heart-warming. From a business perspective, this is a repeatable framework I can and will use over and over again, that will allow us to better forecast revenue and grow our company. After this last launch, I instantly put two job postings up and focused on growing my team to do this bigger and better next time around."

Website: theleveragedpractice.com
Instagram: @theleveragedpractice
Facebook Group: Leverage Your Practice

Tatiana Amico

Business Coach
$42k in two launches

Ideal Client: An online business owner who is feeling stuck and unhappy in her business. She is making some money but wants to grow it to six figures and beyond. She feels overwhelmed and knows what she needs is help, specifically coaching on mindset and how to stand out.

The Offer: Tatiana's offer was a six-month program at $3,500.

Facebook Group: Tatiana grew her group to 250 without ads in about a week and a half. She didn't have help for her first two launches.

Tatiana had been relying on social media posting for sales. The Live Launch Method gave her a simple process to close multiple sales at once.

Comments: "The Live Launch Method reminded me of the power of truly connecting with my audience – the excitement of being on live with them and helping them! It feels like I'm truly helping my people and creating shifts in them!"

Instagram: @tatianaamico
Facebook Group: Your Next Level Business Society

Rachel Lee

Online Business Coaching and Strategy
$75k in predictable revenue

Ideal Client: Rachel's ideal clients are coaches, consultants, and course creators.

The Offer: IMPACT coaching program, a business incubator with a cost of $5,000 for 12 months of access.

Facebook Group: Rachel had a large Facebook group of 6,000 but started this launch with a pop-up group and went from zero to 750 in four weeks. She used DMs to invite members and spent $450 in ads to reach her ideal client. Her profitable team consisted of social sellers, VAs, a copywriter, and an ad specialist.

Prior to the Live Launch Method, Rachel didn't have a consistent sales system in place. She would sell randomly via live stream but didn't create predictable revenue for herself until joining The Unstoppable Entrepreneur. During her live launch, she was able to add 15 people to her business using the Live Launch Method.

Comments: "An indoctrination process like this really works, but you have to put the work in. Each time you do it, it will get easier and easier. Try to do as many as possible."

Website: Rachelslee.com
Instagram: @rachelsleedotcom
Facebook: Facebook.com/rachellee707

Ann Strout

Sales Ninja and Business Mentor
This has been a game changer for me

Ideal Client: Coaches and service-based entrepreneurs who want to scale online, sell with soul, and impact globally.

The Offer: Ann offered her 12-month Profitable Entrepreneur coaching and implementation program.

Facebook Group: Ann has used launches before working with me, but the *system* taught *behind* the Live Launch Method was new to her and a true game changer.

Her previous Facebook group of 1,500 was not engaging the right audience, so she deleted and started from scratch for this live launch. It took her about a month to add 500 new members organically through DMs, and in the end, she gained 30 new clients.

Comments: "My wow moment came when I realized how easy launching can be when you focus on mastering the same system over and over and funneling prospects into a program that is your flagship! I have always collaborated to grow my business and authority in this industry, and bringing that into my launches has made a *huge* difference as I was the only one filling my programs before. Now I have massive buzz around my own launch and paid program by building an audience who believes in it as much as I do. Business simplified right there.

"It's been game changer to the way I think about launching and the system I use to actually do the launch. My positioning is different, my ideal client is different, my brand is different, and my income is different."

Website: annkeaney.com
Instagram: www.instagram.com/_annkeaney/
Facebook: www.facebook.com/annkeaneyofficial/
Facebook: www.facebook.com/AnnKeaneyCoaching/

Cindy Kennedy

Life & Leadership Coaching for Women
Now it is easy to share my program offer

Ideal Client: Cindy's ideal clients are women with bold dreams who want to get out of the way of their own success and answer the calling deep within to share their gifts, stories, and services with the world. They are ambitious professionals and heart-centered entrepreneurs, between the ages of 35-55 who are serious about reconnecting to what really matters to them and turn their vision into action and gifts into impact.

The Offer: Rise to Shine leadership accelerator program to pave the way for women with bold dreams to speak up, stand out, and shine – nine-month program priced at $7,650 Australian. This was her second launch. The first time, she offered a six-week program for $1,997.

Facebook Group: Cindy started using the Live Launch Method because she wanted to expand the reach of her teachings and impact online. This was completely new territory for her, and the organic connection is what drew her to this method. She started her launch with 254 Facebook group members and is adding to her group daily with a goal of reaching 300 soon. Cindy spent $700 on Facebook ads, using a VA for social media posting, Facebook outreach planning and tracking.

The Live Launch Method has kickstarted her business online. Not only does she have some visibility from women across seven different countries, but it has propelled her to bring much of her intellectual property, which has really helped her shape what she stands for, who she serves, and what her true strengths are.

It has given her the cash flow to build her signature program and pay for experts to support her in this along with massive growth in business as well as confidence in terms of tangibly experiencing the value of her work from women across the globe.

Cindy's first launch brought in over $23k, and she has since raised her price for her next launch!

Comments: "My gift is the ability to build deep connections quickly with clients and groups face to face, and I wasn't sure if this would translate online. Was I ever wrong! The Live Launch Method is set up to build and deepen connection over time. This became evident when participants not only engaged with me throughout the lessons (which I really need!) but with each other. To see them comment and support and elevate each other (once strangers from other countries and now sharing a growth experience due to shared need) allowed for a unique learning environment to unfold."

Website: www.cindymkennedy.com
Instagram and Facebook: @cindymkennedy
LinkedIn: @cindy-m-kennedy

Jessica Barnak – Barnak International, LLC

Business Coaching
Over $100k in two launches

Ideal Client: Female entrepreneurs who are new to business (one to three years) and struggling to focus, both in strategy and in mindset. They are "firehosing" their clients – throwing everything at them to see what sticks, but nothing is working because they don't have focus, simplicity, or consistency. They are also allowing fears, limitations, and overwhelm prevent them from taking action.

The Offer: The Founders Academy is a six-month hybrid coaching program that teaches new entrepreneurs how to find clarity, develop a high-ticket flagship offer, simplify their visibility on social media, generate new leads consistently, and move past the mindset blocks that hold them back from taking action. The program is $650 a month for six months.

Facebook Group: Jessica needed something that was rinse-repeat and easy to try on her own the first time. She wasn't at a place where she could afford a team to help her, and the Live Launch Method felt simple. Her entire business is built on simplicity and flexing around her children, so this was the perfect strategy for her to not only get results but practice what she preaches.

Jessica started her Facebook group for her live launch and in two weeks had 300 members. She was at 1,000 members within about three months using organic growth methods.

Admittedly, her first live launch didn't seem overwhelmingly successful because it was new and she was nervous; she had five people join the program. But her **second** launch was when things started getting good, and she ended up with 14 new students in their program at $650/month. Since then, she has been consistently closing at a four to six percent conversion rate every time she launches the program.

Comments: "I have always tried to *serve* my audience from a place of genuine concern for their journey in business and in life, and the Live Launch Method really gave me the process to not only serve them but to easily and effectively take the relationship to the next level where I'm paid well for what I do. Most entrepreneurs are terrified of selling – of that transition to making the offer – and I was too in the beginning. I was uncomfortable making that offer. The Live Launch Method not only made me extremely comfortable with that process of saying, "Isn't this fun? Let's work together," but it also helps me show my clients that it's okay if they sell too."

Website: www.jessicabarnak.com
Instagram: @spiritualbosses

Debbie Cherry – Freedom Practitioner

Business Coaching
$96k in sales

Ideal Client: An innovative clinician who is sick of the medical model and wants way more freedom, flexibility, fulfillment, and fun!

The Offer: Freedom Practitioner Transformation – 12-month program for $8k in which she walks courageous therapists through the path to own, love, share, package, and sell their gifts, so they can engage and enroll clients they absolutely *love* working with.

Facebook Group: Debbie started her live launch with an existing Facebook group of 4,000 who were active but many were not engaged before her launch. They just stirred up the people they already had and added 300 members in two weeks, organically. She had a team of two very part-time VA-type people who helped with messaging and tagging. Debbie added 12 new clients through her live launch via consult calls, for $96k in sales.

Comments: "It's such a better way to bring people into your program... they have a huge running head start and so much trust, so clients get even better results in less time."

Website: www.debbiecherry.com
Facebook: www.facebook.com/debbie.rackoff.cherry

Jaime Lynn Curely – The Tailor Made Life

Network Marketing
The live launch for network marketing

Ideal Client: Jaime Lynn's ideal customer is someone ready to make a change in their health! She loves working with busy women, mainly moms.

The Offer: Jaime Lynn and her network marketing team invited prospects to join them for a 30-day reset! The price point varied based on specific goals and budget of each person but on average is $300 per month.

Facebook Group: Jaime Lynn loves educating others on how important nutrition is to living a healthy balanced lifestyle, and the Live Launch Method proved to be a great way to do that. When she started, her group consisted of 245 members. Her team all worked together to invite their own prospects to the group via DMs, and after two weeks, added 35 new members. They offered offline conversations and a Q&A in the group, with a direct link to sign up for recurring packages through their company.

Comments: "This is so duplicatable for our team! As a professional in the network marketing industry, I know that success is 10 percent me and 90 percent duplication. The Live Launch Method allows my team to come together, so we can all educate and eventually support our customers!"

Website: thetailormadelife.isagenix.com/guide
Instagram: jaimelynncurley
Facebook Group: Confidence Catwalk

Carly Wilson & Lyndie Davis – Your Best Foot Forward

Group Mindset Coaching

$10K+ launch weeks after joining The Unstoppable Entrepreneur

Ideal Client: Female entrepreneurs working a side hustle, struggling with mindset and ready to level-up.

The Offer: 12-week group coaching program that Includes ten modules, a weekly masterclass with actionable assignments, two weekly group accountability/Q&A zooms, two monthly private calls (included in the price for initial launch only as a bonus). The cost of their offer was $947 paid in full or three payments of $347.

Facebook Group: When they joined The Unstoppable Entrepreneur, they had 100 people in a Facebook group that they had been nurturing. It took them two weeks to get the group size to 300 using our DM strategy without ads.

Carly and Lyndie took fast action. After just a few weeks in The Unstoppable Entrepreneur program, they were deep in the throes of their live launch. They didn't even have a sales page, and still don't! Despite having a serious case of imposter syndrome, they pushed forward and serviced their people. After the very first day, they realized how much their audience needed what they were offering and doing a launch this way increased their confidence significantly. They had no idea what to expect since they had never launched a program before, so they were pleasantly surprised to have 11 people sign up for over $10k in sales.

As soon as they completed their launch, they were ready to go for another round. There was no stress, anxiety, or overwhelm. They were simply able to connect with the women who needed them in an incredibly powerful way and add over $10k to their bank accounts while doing that.

Comments: "We know we have more to give and that there are so many others out there searching for us. Our belief in what we're doing has skyrocketed because of the Live Launch Method."

Facebook Group: Your Best Foot Forward - #yourbff

Elizabeth Caputo – 4D Associates International

Personal and Professional Coaching
$14k in sales with a group of 112 people

Ideal Client: Women and men who want to become certified coaches or executives/entrepreneurs who want to enhance their communication and relationship skills.

The Offer: Elizabeth created a special offer of $2,945 instead of $3,465 for a limited time or the option with a payment plan option of $396/month instead of $495. Her program lasts from 6 - 12 months depending on the flexibility of the participant.

Facebook Group: Elizabeth was inspired by The Live Launch Method and decided to give it a try. She personally loves training people, so being able to sell online was what attracted her to starting her Facebook group. She was able to build her group from zero to 112 group members organically within four days. She currently has 180 active members in her group. Her team consists of a few friends who have been willing to help her along the way. During her live launch, she added six new clients.

Comments: "The Live Launch Method allowed me to start being more visible and to start structuring the program, the offer, and the marketing strategy in the most effective way. On a more personal level, training to become a Certified Transformational Coach is also a personal transformational experience. My wow moment was found in the power of serving others by helping them with the most valuable goal in life – having the best relationships they can have."

Website: www.4dcertification.com
Instagram: @elylaracaputo
Facebook: www.facebook.com/caputoely

Melissa Barrios

Online Marketing
I was blown away by all the engagement!

Ideal Client: Spanish-speaking women living in the U.S. between 30-45 years old in the early stages of entrepreneurship who are looking to build and scale an online business and achieve freedom and flexibility.

The Offer: The Instagram Master Plan: an eight-week program to help clients leverage Instagram and convert followers into clients. The price point was $437.

Facebook Group: Melissa started her Facebook group with 250 members and was able to grow her group to 550 using $90 of Facebook ads. Melissa, working on her own, added five new clients for her program through a direct link sign up.

Melissa believes the Live Launch Method was a much more elegant way to launch, and she loved that it helped build trust and connection with cold leads.

Comments: "I was blown away by all the engagement and positive feedback my live sessions had. I wasn't expecting so many people to show up and interact with the content like they did."

Website: www.melissaberrios.net/
Instagram: @melissamberrios
Facebook Group: Virtualmente Libre

Jenny C Tse – Sipping Streams Tea Company

Food and Beverage
It forced me to create a program that I am passionate about!

Ideal Client: Women ages 30-55 interested in health and wellness and tea.

The Offer: Jenny's offer was the Sipping Streams Subscription Box program that she created for this live launch. Members can choose to pay monthly ($45) or yearly ($450).

Facebook Group: Jenny started her launch with 115 existing Facebook members and she grew her group to 300 in two weeks, organically. Jenny had a 20 percent conversion rate and was able to add 20 subscribers for her new offer.

Comments: "The Live Launch Method forced me to create a program that I am passionate about and brought in income to support what I am interested in doing. I was surprised that it worked and that I made any sales at all! And most importantly, it motivated me in creating a better program for my company that complemented my strengths in teaching and encouraging health and wellness through tea."

Website: www.sippingstreams.com
Instagram: @sippingstreams
Facebook: @sippingstreams

Courtney R Zentz – Tiny Transitions

Pediatric Sleep Coaching
Trust the process.

Ideal Client: Parents of children who struggle with sleep needs, habits, and abilities.

The Offer: Courtney's offer was a consultation to work with her in a private coaching capacity. Her current packages start at $695, but she is in the process of launching a scalable, access-based program at a higher price for a longer duration in 2020.

Facebook Group: Courtney started her Facebook group for her live launch and it took about three months for her to reach 300 members using a combination of organic marketing and Facebook ads. She spent less than $500 on her ads. Her team consisted of one VA and one intern who helped with her launch.

As a result, Courtney is seeing double growth now every month, and she is able to focus on this full-time, whereas before it was merely a side hustle. She is excited to see it grow into what she knows it can in the future. During her live launch she added six new clients through consult calls.

Comments: "Kelly and her unique approach to the market has changed how I now engage with potential clients through the Live Launch Method. I love the community I have built, of parents supporting each other on their journey to sleep, while I provide education and the foundation to achieve their unique family goals.

"I have learned to trust the process and when you show value, people buy."

Website: www.tinytransitions.com

Instagram: @Tiny_Transitions_Sleep_Coach
Facebook: www.facebook.com/tinytransitions
TikTok: @TinyTransitions

Marcia Bench – Spiritual Women Entrepreneurs Institute

Coaching & Training

I booked more sales in this one live launch than <u>anything</u> else I've done in 30 years in business.

Ideal Client: Marcia's ideal clients are spiritually guided women entrepreneurs in service businesses such as coaching, energy work, and the like.

The Offer: Marcia offered the Divine & Aligned Biz Builders program, $9k paid in full or $897/month for one year.

Facebook Group: Marcia started her live launch with an existing Facebook group of 320 members. She used DMs and messaging to grow and strengthen her group with the help of a VA who posted, sent DMs, and tagged for her within the group.

During her first live launch with her new company, Marcia added six new clients. Due to the price point of her package, she booked $58k in sales with $10k of that money she could bank.

Comments: "Despite the fact that (or due to Divine Order I think!) my launch scheduled weeks ago, happened during the COVID-19 outbreak, I booked $38k in sales on a *Saturday* in this environment. WOW! I don't know of another strategy I could use to do that… from home, in my comfy clothes, online, and make a difference in people's lives.

"I booked more sales in this one live launch than *anything* else I've done in 30 years in business, 19 of them online. I feel like now I have a strategy I can rinse and repeat over and over, adding ads to amplify the results, and feel confident I can grow my program to 100 or more members by the end of the year. And my dream of owning a million-dollar business is now within reach (probably in 2021)."

Website: spiritualwomenentrepreneursinstitute.com
Facebook Group: Divine and Aligned Women Entrepreneurs
LinkedIn: marciabench

Sirli Sillasoo – Elukirg OÜ

Coaching
My business went from a standstill to thriving overnight!

Ideal Client: Sirli's ideal client is a woman who has that one specific dream in her heart that she needs to bring into the world by writing her book, traveling, or moving to her dream country, finding that dream job or a partner, starting her dream business, etc.

The Offer: Sirli's offer was to join a 12-month program at 119€ per month for the Estonian market.

Facebook Group: Sirli started her live launch with an existing group of 1,574 people. The group had been cold for two years. She used Facebook ads and spent 200€ to bring in some new people.

She did two launches back-to-back. Sirli opened her cart on the same day Estonia declared the emergency situation due to the Coronavirus, and since she felt the world had just changed so rapidly, she did the launch again two weeks later. First time, she was on her own, and the second time she had a little help with her Facebook group tagging and some DMs. She was able to add 22 new coaching clients during both of her live launches.

Comments: "I loved the social selling part of my live launch. I had so many great conversations going on with people when previously I didn't like to sell at all. When using Kelly's methods, it didn't feel like I was selling but just connecting with people who were interested and who resonated with what I was teaching. Live launches and the structure that Kelly teaches transformed my business overnight from a standstill into a thriving business, and all of that after the global pandemic had hit the world. I started my business from scratch after a burnout two years ago and made $26K in sales within a month!"

Website: sirlisillasoo.com
Facebook: CoachSirliSillasoo
Facebook Group: Elukirglikud - Estonian group

Ciara Stockeland – Ciara Stockeland

Coach for Boutique Owners
A great platform to get my message in front of customers.

Ideal Client: Boutique owners

The Offer: Ciara offered three months of coaching at $347/month.

Facebook Group: Ciara started her Facebook group for the live launch and it took her two months to reach 300 members, organically. She conducted 20 consult calls and added 12 clients for her coaching program as a result of her live launch.

Ciara closed $12k in sales on her very first launch, while being able to purposefully encourage and share her message with a community of her ideal clients!

Comments: "It provides a great platform to get my message in front of customers."

Website: www.ciarastockeland.com
Instagram: @cstockeland
Facebook Group: Powerfully Simple Business Tribe

Shelley Riutta – Global Association of Holistic Psychotherapy and Coaching

Business Coaching for Holistic Professionals and Holistic Life Coaching Certification Training Programs
I feel like I'm living my fullest vision and potential for my business.

Ideal Client: Shelley's ideal clients are therapists, healers, coaches, and health practitioners who practice holistically.

The Offer: Shelley's offer was the Holistic Business School 12-month Program for $5K and Holistic Business School Premiere, which includes Holistic Life Coach Certification Training Program 12 months for $8,500.

Facebook Group: Shelley started with 250 existing Facebook members, and it took her about two months to reach 300 members. During her first live launch, she grew her group organically and added Facebook ads for her next two launches. Shelley's team consisted of a VA and a social seller.

She added 25 new clients during her live launches for well over six figures in sales.

Her live launch experience totally transformed her business and has put it on a powerful path of exponential growth. They signed the most amazing, committed clients who are on fire and getting incredible results. The group is abuzz with powerful, forward movement and are singing Shelley's and her team's praises. She couldn't be more thrilled with what is happening.

Comments: "I loved being on the receiving end of the live launch – it was authentic, relational, and transformative and inspired me to want to do it in my own business. It is a powerful, immersive experience for potential clients that ends up powerfully drawing your ideal clients to sign on as clients.

"I feel like I am living my fullest potential and vision for my business and supporting my Clients to do the same!

"The magic and transformation that happens during the live launch is beyond anything I have ever experienced in my business over the last nine years. It is hard to put into words how powerful and impactful it has been for me, my clients, and my business. It is pure magic!!"

Website: thegahp.com
Twitter: @shelleyriutta
Facebook Group: Tribe of Holistic Professionals

Conclusion

The Live Launch Method was born out of my extreme frustration that came from the overly complicated and ineffective launch strategies all the gurus were teaching. My lack of success with those methods led to a huge realization: There was a major need in the market for a simplified way to leverage human connection and remove the barriers between entrepreneurs and their prospects. This led to the creation of the Live Launch Method which is based on the timeless business principle of service being the primary vehicle of sales.

My team and I have spent countless hours perfecting this process, improving the experience for workshop attendees, and teaching our clients how to leverage this methodology. While it took thousands of wasted dollars on things that didn't work, countless precious hours, and plenty of blood, sweat, and tears to get to where we are today, I couldn't be more grateful.

As a company, we've used the Live Launch Method to scale our business to the multiple-seven-figure mark and will hit eight figures by the end of this year. While we are thrilled with our own results, the most rewarding part of this process is without a doubt, the stories that follow this conclusion.

In the coming pages. you will read case study after case study of clients who have used the Live Launch Method to scale their businesses in incredible ways. These people come from all walks of life, from all over the globe, and from various industries. They were all looking for ways to break past their income plateaus, connect with their people, and find some freedom in their lives and business. The Live Launch Method has allowed them to do all of those things. Their stories are a true testament not only to the Live Launch Method and the power of the Unstoppable Entrepreneur program but to the value of perseverance and hard work. Many of these clients had to overcome multiple failures to reach the success they are experiencing today. Their resilience and grit combined with the right strategy and support have skyrocketed their success.

The Live Launch Method is undoubtedly the most effective and simplest launch strategy on the planet. However, I won't lie to you saying it doesn't take any work. Of course, there is work involved, but the work you put in will have an exponentially greater return than you could ever imagine! The clients featured in the following section are the ones who did the work. They are the ones who made no excuses, saw the golden ticket standing in front of them (in the form of the live launch) and took that golden ticket straight to the bank.

Today, countless lives have been changed thanks to the Live Launch Method, and we couldn't be more thrilled to see the fruits of our labor make such an incredible impact.

Eventually, platforms will change and tactics will have to be revisited. However, the core tenets of the Live Launch Method will remain: human connection, simplicity, service, and intuition. No algorithm can override the power of these things, and our clients inside the Unstoppable Entrepreneur will have the skillset, tools and support they need to pivot.

If you are reading this book and have made it this far, you are probably one of the few committed entrepreneurs out there willing to do the work it takes to build a truly global brand. I want to encourage you to implement what we've outlined here and commit to mastering it. Join us inside the Tribe of Unstoppables to watch how we run our launches and be sure to subscribe to Unstoppable Entrepreneur Radio on iTunes, so you can stay up-to-date on the real time data we are getting from our own launches.

Before I go, I want to encourage you with this: There is no limit to what you can achieve using the Live Launch Method and no limit to the impact you can make when you choose to fill the gap and serve in a way no one else is willing to serve. Yes, a large percentage of our clients have consistent six-figure launches due to the Live Launch Method, but more importantly, they are enjoying the process, building their brands, and making a real and lasting impact on the people they serve. The same opportunity is available to you. Do the work, implement what we teach, commit to mastery, and stay connected with Team Unstoppable. If you do those four things, I am willing to bet a large sum of money that you will see an incredible return on your investment!

About the Author

Kelly Roach transforms overworked entrepreneurs into seven-figure CEOs. With her Executive Fortune 500 experience and results, Kelly combines timeless business principles employed by billion-dollar corporations with the speed and agility of the most powerful online marketing strategies of today.

Kelly's company, the Unstoppable Entrepreneur is the leading online business coaching program in North America today. Leveraging scalable intimacy to create the first-ever accountability-driven coaching program on the market, while revolutionizing the way entrepreneurs launch their offers, Kelly's company has catapulted into the multi-millions while helping entrepreneurs around the globe do the same.

In addition to being a best-selling author, Kelly is also an ongoing expert on ABC, NBC, Fox, and The CW. She has been featured in some of the world's leading publications including *Inc.* and *Forbes* and is the host of the Top 50 Marketing podcast, "The Unstoppable Entrepreneur Show."

Kelly is committed to ongoing philanthropic work, with a 1:1 business model that brings clean drinking water to those who do not have access through her Human Family Foundation.

In addition to running her coaching company with a team of 20 full-time employees (and growing), Kelly is the co-founder of a second company, Give Her Courage, The Courageous Brand. Kelly founded this company to create a movement designed to give young girls the competitive edge they need to rise to the top, break through barriers, and create lasting change in the world.

The Unstoppable Entrepreneur website:
www.uerevolution.com

The Unstoppable Entrepreneur Show:
www.kellyroachcoaching.com/podcast

Connect with Kelly:

Facebook: @unstoppableentrepreneurshow
Facebook Community: Tribe of Unstoppables
Instagram: @Kellyroachofficial
LinkedIn: @Kelly Roach

    To learn how you can work with Kelly and her team, email Stephanie@kellyroachcoaching.com or visit www.kellyroachcoaching.com.